NATURE, CONTEMPLATION,

AND THE ONE

Nature, Contemplation, and the One

A Study in the Philosophy of Plotinus

John N. Deck

PUBLISHED FOR THE PAUL BRUNTON
PHILOSOPHIC FOUNDATION BY

LARSON PUBLICATIONS

Originally published in 1967 by
University of Toronto Press

International Standard Book Number: 0-943914-54-X
Library of Congress Catalogue Card Number: 91–72199

Manufactured in the United States of America

Published for the
Paul Brunton Philosophic Foundation by
Larson Publications
4936 State Route 414
Burdett, NY 14818

95 94 93 92 91
10 9 8 7 6 5 4 3 2 1

TO MY WIFE

CONTENTS

JOHN DECK philosophized and taught philosophy in Windsor, Ontario, just across the river from downtown Detroit. Each summer for at least twenty years, I would spend about a week with him, telling stories and playing bridge with all the family in the evenings, philosophizing as we walked the streets of Windsor (stopping occasionally for coffee, or for lunch at a favorite spot) during the day. We talked metaphysics, but for us—as for those great thinkers we most respected, that meant going to the roots of questions concerning ethics, education, the destiny of the human being, the creation of the universe, and God. Being both of us believing Catholics, we took up the perennial task of "faith seeking understanding."

Both of us had learned to philosophize in schools influenced (in a quite immediate way) by Etienne Gilson and Jacques Maritain, and that meant that while our quest was philosophical, it took the form of communion, conversation, with great philosophers of times past—Parmenides, Plato, Aristotle, Plotinus, Augustine, Thomas Aquinas, Descartes, Hume, Hegel—as well as present-day minds. I have always listened most closely, among many philosophical voices, to Thomas Aquinas. John listened to him, too, but he spent much time with Hegel and with Plotinus.

All this I mention to underline the fact, which will soon be evident to the reader, that while John Deck approached Plotinus with all desirable scholarly rigor and technique, he turned to Plotinus as to a living mind, one of the great philosophers with whom we have the possibility and the privilege to enter into philosophical friendship and discipleship. For us, learning to philosophize was a true apprenticeship. We lived in the company of the greats, and we did, along with them, the things they did. As one sees a painting "from the workshop of Fra Angelico," so also our papers, our conversations, might have been labelled: "from the workshop of Plotinus."

This will also help explain to the reader why there is not a long list of books by John Deck. Writing, it is true, did not come easily for him. Still, that is not, I would say, the principal reason. Speaking of the poem of Parmenides (written about 480 B.C.), Heidegger, in his Introduction to Metaphysics, says something to the effect that those who have appreciated the depth and power of its few lines must lose all desire to write books.

Be that as it may, John Deck made his truly Socratic presence felt among a few generations of students and colleagues at the University of Windsor. His funeral in 1979 was remarkable for the large number of former students who attended, from all walks of life, but among them many teachers.

Plotinus was not just a book for John Deck. And I am, as John's literary executor, most happy that Paul Cash and Larson Publications have chosen to make this work more readily available. I feel sure that those who read it will remember with me the words of Walt Whitman:

> This is no book, camarado.
> Who touches this touches a man!

LAWRENCE DEWAN, O.P.
Dominican College of Philosophy
and Theology
Ottawa, Canada

PUBLISHER'S PREFACE TO THE 1991 EDITION

WE ARE delighted to re-issue this magnificent book, widely recognized as one of the best books ever written about the philosophy of Plotinus.

With Plotinus becoming—both as an achieved philosopher and as a fulfilled mystic—increasingly inspiring to modern spiritual seekers, it is essential to make the best studies of his work readily available to readers who are not Greek specialists. As a step toward that end, we have made this edition more visually accessible by transliterating the Greek characters of the original version. Beyond that, our only changes have been to correct a number of typos in the original.

Most significant of these changes are substituting the word "change" for "chance" in the fourth sentence of footnote 4 in chapter 3, and changing the word "casual" to "causal" in the third paragraph from the end of chapter 10.

We are most grateful to Father Lawrence Dewan, John Deck's literary executor, for his enthusiastic cooperation in making this fine book available for a new generation. We are also profoundly grateful to Anthony Damiani for introducing us to this book, and for awakening us to the immeasurable value of Plotinus' contributions to the spiritual legacy of the modern world.

"NATURE contemplates." My concern in this book has been to provide a setting in which a modern reader can understand and evaluate this doctrine—a doctrine which has close connections with all the principal themes of Plotinus' philosophy, and which cannot be explained without bringing them into play. I have tried first to give a sufficiently elaborate presentation of "nature as a contemplator" within Plotinus' technical conceptual framework, and then to consider more broadly its philosophic import.

In seeking to make Plotinus' thought readily accessible to an English-speaking audience, one is faced with the absence of a good, complete English translation. The MacKenna translation, even in its revised edition, is inexact. There are several scholarly translations of excerpts, but I have found grounds for questioning the accuracy of some of their renderings. For these reasons, and for the sake of general uniformity, the translations used, both in the body of the book and in the notes and appendix, are my own. I have been helped by the work of numerous other translators—in particular, I have found helpful the Latin translation done by the Renaissance Platonist, Marsilio Ficino.

It has seemed to me of slight value to categorize Plotinus' philosophy by "ism" words, which can mean many things to as many people. I have made only incidental references to his supposed idealism, rationalism, etc., either initially or in my conclusions.

Certain Greek words, which seemed insusceptible of translation by single words or short phrases, but which have been employed frequently in the text, have been rendered in Roman orthography. These words are:

θεωρία	theoria (pl. theoriai)
λόγος	logos (pl. logoi)
ποίησις	poiesis (adj. poietic)
οὐσία	ousia
συναίσθησις	synesthesis
θεώρημα	theorema (pl. theoremata)
νόημα	noema (pl. noemata)
νόησις	noesis (pl. noeseis)
λογισμός	logismos
διανοία	dianoia
πρᾶξις	praxis
φύσις	physis
σύνεσις	synesis

I have used occasionally the adjective "ontic" and the adverb "ontically." They are to be understood as meaning the same as the clumsy "being-ish" and "being-ly"; they are not intended to convey any reference or allusion to any specialized meaning they may have for certain contemporary philosophers.

Thanks to Porphyry, Plotinus' pupil, friend, and literary executor, we have a list of Plotinus' treatises which gives their chronological order, but not their exact dates. There is reason to doubt, however, that chronological considerations should be a controlling factor in attempting to understand Plotinus.

Plotinus wrote no systematic account of his philosophy. The *Enneads* collect the detached treatises of a thinker and teacher who began writing only when he was fifty years old, and whose literary activity was confined to the seventeen or eighteen years he still had to live. Many of the treatises exhibit a close connection with his schoolroom lecturing. An individual treatise, although rhetorically self-contained, may not give Plotinus' last or most profound word on the subject with which it deals. In some cases we may have two treatises on the same subject at two different didactic levels. The chronologically prior is in some cases doctrinally more profound. Given such a situation, it seemed to me better to approach the treatises with an eye to possible indications of a well worked-out, coherent philosophy, than to look from the outset for surprising reversals, or revolutionary developments in Plotinus' doctrine from treatise to treatise. Thus I have not viewed *prima facie* the treatise "On Nature, Contemplation, and the One" (number 30 in the chronological order), which forms the background of this book, as a new departure, even though some doctrines are stated explicitly only in this treatise. Rather, I have tried to see it as a well integrated part of Plotinus' overall philosophy. In point of fact its doctrines might well have comprised the subject of many lectures which were not recorded during the years in which Plotinus taught but did not publish.

It is superficial to look immediately upon any philosopher as the automatic resultant of the literary forces operating upon him. We must see the exact state in which notions and doctrines, which he may share or appear to share with earlier philosophers, appear in his philosophy, and this can be done only by attending to the actual features of his notions and shadings of notions. A cautious treatment of real or supposed sources and developments is required; we may not assume at the outset that Plotinus represents an inconsistent amalgam of Plato, Aristotle, the Stoics, the Middle Platonists, traces of Christianity (via his teacher, Ammonius Saccas), and perhaps even "oriental influences." It is true that Plotinus, like many other philosophers, borrows much of his vocabulary, and even elements of his conceptual apparatus, from many sources. But it seems to me beyond doubt that he had a fresh, personal grasp of reality, and that he had his own controlling notions, under the direction of which he reworked and reinterpreted his sources and so achieved an internal unity in his thought. Clearly, there can be no *a priori* demonstration that any philosophic writer is more than a syncretist: but if it is good to keep our eyes open to spot "sources," it is even better to bear in mind that a philosopher is one who sees *things*, and to be ready to appreciate it when sources are handled uniquely and, in fact, transmuted.

To attend to what Plotinus exactly says means more than to give a doxographical report of what are, or what appear to be, his doctrines. Plotinus' own mode of presentation suggests the procedures which can give a valid insight into his meaning. His philosophy does not, generally speaking, contain demonstrations in Aristotle's sense of the word. Nor do his writings, in most cases, seem to reproduce any genuine avenue of discovery. Because of didactic exigencies, or because of the actual sequence of his thought—and probably because of both—his treatises appear as elaborations and clarifications of preconceived notions. Often they are inductions into, or carefully constructed familiarizations with, a primary insight which he appears to possess all along. His presentation, and probably also his thought, is "spiral" rather than linear. In many places he does not so much prove his propositions and notions as accustom his hearers and readers to their truth. The result is that it often seems that he is proving conclusions by premises and premises by conclusions, when in fact he is elaborating an intuition, building up its specific conceptual apparatus, connecting it with other parts of his thought, and rendering it plausible and acceptable. But his "intuition" is commonly rooted in reality, and there is in most cases no reason to suppose that it comes from thin air, or from some unique (and incommunicable) experience.

In the effort to understand and interpret Plotinus it is necessary to adopt many perspectives, and to move eventually, as the thought warrants, to synthesis and simultaneity. It will be seen that many apparent definitions, categorical propositions, and distinctions cannot stand as such when compared with other texts. But this in itself does not point to inconsistency; it means simply that the reader of Plotinus is confronted with modifications and adjustments which, while possibly present simultaneously to the philosopher's mind, are presented sequentially for exegesis. Statements made at the beginning, therefore, must always be held open for possible reinterpretation.

I wish to express my thanks to Dr. Anton C. Pegis of the Pontifical Institute of Mediaeval Studies and the University of Toronto, who first interested me in Plotinus; to the Rev. Joseph Owens of the same institutions for many valuable suggestions; to my friends and colleagues Dr. John Glanville, Dr. Joseph Graham, and Mr. Robert Pinto for historical, philosophical, and editorial assistance; to Miss M. Jean Houston and Mr. Jan Schreiber of the University of Toronto Press, the latter of whom gave the manuscript its most thorough and penetrating reading; and to Mrs. Wesley Wade for typing (and re-typing) it.

Publication of this book has been assisted both by a grant from the Humanities Research Council of Canada using funds provided by the Canada Council, and by the Publications Fund of the University of Toronto Press.

1

FOR MANY modern readers of Plotinus, *Ennead* III, 8, "On Nature, Contemplation, and the One," has seemed worthy of special attention. It stands out for its finished literary execution, for its weaving together of central Plotinian themes, and for its unification of the Plotinian world by a contemplation present in all things below the One, the Plotinian God. It impresses equally those who see Plotinus as a mystic and look to him perhaps for guidance in non-Christian religious experiences, and those who see him as a philosopher, as the last great representative of the Greek tradition.

Ennead III, 8, begins with a teaching that is, and is meant to be, novel and striking. Nature contemplates. The nature in trees, plants, and the earth contemplates. Further, nature produces trees, plants, and the earth by contemplating. Contemplation is thus productive—productive of concrete, substantial realities.

To examine Plotinus' doctrine of "nature as a contemplator" thoroughly will mean to reappraise his whole philosophy. For this doctrine, arresting though it is on its own account, sets the stage for the development in the immediately succeeding chapters of III, 8, in which Plotinus traces contemplation through the familiar three hypostases of his "system" (the Soul, the Intelligence, and the One), apparently equating contemplation with the producing of the inferior in each case, except that of the One (III, 8, 5–11). Nature, the lower "part" of the World Soul, has itself been produced by the contemplative activity of the World Soul proper. The World Soul has been produced, it would seem, by the contemplative activity of the Nous (the Intelligence, the Knower). Only the One, which is beyond the duality of knowledge, seemingly does not contemplate, and produces the Nous in a different way. In all other instances, producing comes about through contemplating.

It is obvious that *Ennead* III, 8, gives a fairly complete picture of Plotinus' world, and locates nature-as-contemplation in the lower reaches of that world. Its emphasis on contemplation makes it a relatively fresh and independent picture.[2] Less apparent is the relevance of *Ennead* III, 8, to the real world. The present-day reader, who, regardless of his personal convictions, cannot be indifferent to the influence of popular or philosophic positivism, may well regard Plotinus' concentration upon contemplation as a romantic fantasy. At first glance it may seem that, in making all reality (except the One) contemplative, Plotinus takes the world to be dreamy, inconclusive, insubstantial "thought." In making contemplation productive, he shows a lack of appreciation of production as we see it taking place in the world, by the impact of one material thing on another. In general, we may think that Plotinus seems not to grasp the world as it is, but to remake it according to a highly questionable inward vision. If we like, we may call this mysticism, and perhaps honor it as such, but we will scarcely credit it as a hardheaded attempt to understand the actual world.

To treat *Ennead* III, 8, quite seriously as philosophy we must, however, go beyond "attitudes" towards trees which contemplate—either the attitude of romantic approbation or that of positivistic contempt. We must seek to attain a technical philosophic understanding of what Plotinus sees as contemplation, what he sees as production throughout his world. This will involve an investigation of almost his entire philosophy. And in this investigation we will come upon a doctrine which seems to compromise that of *Ennead* III, 8, 1–4. The production of the vegetative things which come to be in the visible cosmos appears to be effected in a way other than by nature contemplating.

The two treatises "On the Omnipresence of Being" (VI, 4 and 5) present this different view. Here we learn that there is nothing in between matter and the ideas; that the intelligible world (the world of ideas, the Nous) is present to the sensible world; that the sensible world participates in the intelligible world (VI, 4, 2, 17–

49). The chapters in which these doctrines are set forth seem to suggest a lack of mediation between the Nous and matter, and thus can convey the impression that the higher part of the soul, and nature, which have appeared as diminutions from the Nous, are unnecessary and perhaps even impossible intermediaries between the Nous and matter. The entire doctrine seems to be undermined which saw the vegetative things of the visible cosmos as the product of nature's relatively feeble producing-contemplating, which in turn was derived from producing-contemplating by soul, and this in its turn from producing-contemplating by the Nous. What does Plotinus mean? Is the visible universe to be explained as the ultimate product of a series of diminishing hypostases or parts of hypostases, or is it the direct product of the Nous? Which contemplation is really productive of the vegetative things in the cosmos—that of nature or that of the Nous?

It may be possible to see answers to these questions in Plotinus' own texts. Perhaps a co-ordination of the supposedly different doctrines of the producing of the visible cosmos is present in the *Enneads* themselves. But again, what is the philosophic worth of these two doctrines, even if they should turn out to be one? Do they relate to anything that someone who is not a Plotinian initiate experiences or understands? What is Plotinus talking about when he *begins* to treat of nature? Of contemplation? Is he dealing with realities? What is the Nous, the Knower, the "contemplator" in the fullest sense of the term? If Plotinus regards contemplation as productive, does he have any "feel" for producing by hands and tools? Is any continuity traceable between this latter type of producing and contemplative producing?

Then, if it can be admitted that Plotinus' doctrine is worthy of respect as an understandable account of the visible world, does he speak of this world with an undivided voice? If Plotinus is understood as a serious philosopher of the sensible, material world, we seek to know whether he has one ultimate judgement about its production, or two.

NOTES

1. Plotinus, *Ennead* III, treatise 8, chapter 1, lines 18–24. Henceforth such references will be cited in the form III, 8, 4, 18–24. Reference for *Enneads* I–V and for *Ennead* VI, 7, 1–14 is to the edition of Paul Henry and Hans-Rudolph Schwyzer, *Plotini Opera*, I–II (Paris and Brussels, 1951–). For the rest of *Ennead* VI, reference is to the edition of Emile Bréhier, *Plotin Ennéades* (Paris, 1924–1938).

2. Outside of III, 8, contemplation explicitly as such, designated by the noun *theôria* and the cognate *thea*, and expressed by the verb *theôrein*, "contemplate," is mentioned only occasionally. There is a discussion of contemplation in the Nous (V, 3, 5) which parallels that of III, 8, and a fairly extensive treatment of the "contemplation" of the One by the "individual" soul (VI, 9, 11).

2

PLOTINUS' doctrine of the One must be examined for possible primary instances of poiesis and of knowledge. Before treating of the One under these aspects, it is necessary, however, first to
show that the doctrine of the One has a place in Plotinus' philosophy as such, and second to characterize the One more precisely.

For Plotinus, the doctrine of the One appears to be susceptible
of proof. Thus, in the treatise on contemplation, after discussing
the Nous, he argues:

> Such is the Nous. Thus it is not the first, but there must be that
> which is beyond it (our preceding discussion was for the sake of
> this), first of all, because multitude is posterior to one, and mul-
> titude is number, while the One is the principle of number and
> of multitude. And *this* is intelligence and intelligible at once, as
> the two together. If it is two, it is necessary to find (*labein*) what
> is before the two. Now what is it? Nous alone? But to every
> intelligence there is joined an intelligible: for if an intelligible
> is not of necessity joined, there is no intelligence. Now if it is
> not Nous, but escapes the two, that which is prior to these
> two will be beyond Nous. But what prevents it from being the
> intelligible? Because the intelligible, for its part, is yoked to the
> intelligence. But if it is neither intelligence nor intelligible, what
> is it? We shall say that it is that from which come Nous and the
> intelligible which is with it.[1]

This passage has the character of a formal demonstration of the
One. Any multitude is posterior to a *one*. But the Nous, the highest
principle reached so far in the discussion, is a *two*: a duality of

intelligence and intelligible. Therefore, the Nous is posterior to another principle, which is the One.

In a passage closely following this one, Plotinus argues that since the Nous has a need to see and to act, it relates to a higher principle, in respect of which and because of which it sees and acts; this principle is the Good (which is the same as the One).[2]

In both of those proofs the argument proceeds from the lower principle, the Nous; the nature of the Nous is seen to demand the One. The doctrine of the One appears in Plotinus' philosophy by rational exigency.

Therefore, for a philosophic treatment of his doctrines, Plotinus' "mystical" or para-mystical experience of the One may safely be left to one side. Porphyry affirms that his master had such an experience at least four times during his life.[3] Plotinus himself hints at it in several places. For example he says that the soul's "preparation and adornment [for the experience of the One] is evident to those who have prepared themselves" (VI, 7, 34, 11–12); and again, "He who has seen knows what I say, that the soul has another life, when it is towards the One and approaches to the One and participates in it." (VI, 9, 9, 47–49.) But in several places in which he describes the experiencing of the One in terms that seem to go beyond what could be known purely philosophically (V, 3, 17, 26–31; VI, 7, 34, 20–38), he has led up to his remarks by variations on his standard proofs for the One (V, 3, 17, 1–14; VI, 7, 32–33). Thus he has managed his philosophy in such a way that it is quite intelligible as a philosophy—the interpreter need not share, pretend to share, or appreciate Plotinus' mystical experience.

The One, or Good, was demonstrated by the need of the Nous for a principle and a good. The Nous is other than the Good;[4] the caused is other than the cause. The One is thus a distinct hypostasis, a distinct "nature."[5]

Plotinus is at once in difficulty when he begins to describe the One. He sees that for him the One must be ineffable.[6] Even the name "One," if taken as a positive designation, is not suitable (V, 5, 6, 28–30). To add a predicate to the One, or even to say that it is, would be to make it two—"One" and "is"—and therefore the "one which is," the second nature and not the first.

It is called the Good—the Good in the sense that all things, primarily the Nous, desire it,[7] act toward it, act because of it (III, 8, 11, 8–10; VI, 8, 7, 3–6)—are what they are because of it (cf. VI, 7, 23, 18–24) and know by a desire to know it (V, 6, 5, 5–10). It is the good for all things. But does this mean that it is the good for itself? Obviously not, since "good for itself" involves a duality: the Good has no good, since there is nothing beyond it.[8]

And yet the very simplicity of the first principle can be expressed, unless we are merely to repeat endlessly "The One," only by words and phrases which in themselves connote duality. Plotinus is fully aware of this. His tactic is to employ the dualistic phrases, but usually to correct them, usually to remind his hearers that these phrases must be purged of dualism to apply to the One.

Thus VI, 8, 13–18, the longest passage in which Plotinus allows himself the luxury of speaking of the One in dualistic terms, opens and closes with a warning. He is about to speak incorrectly (ouk orthôs), with the purpose of persuading, and must use words which depart from the rigor of knowledge (paranoêteon en tois logois) (VI, 8, 13, 1–5; 47–50). He has had to speak in this way because he has been unable to speak as he would wish (VI, 8, 18, 52–53). In other places, he characteristically prefixes a hoion, or another qualifying phrase or particle, to the dualistic expression.

Speaking "incorrectly," the One is from itself[9] and through itself (VI, 8, 14, 42), it is towards itself,[10] it wills itself (VI, 8, 13, 38–40), it makes or constitutes itself.[11] None of these phrases can mean that the One is in some rapport with itself, as though it were dual. Rather, they express—what? The self-sufficiency[12] of the One? This expression is itself dual. They express the One.

Plotinus says constantly that the One needs nothing.[13] It does not need subsistence, entity, act, or life. If it needed any of these it would not be the first: some other principle, towards which it tended, would supply them to it (cf. III, 8, 11, 38–44). Nor does it have them. For in having them, it would be two: itself, and that which it had. Neither needing them nor having them, but the source from which they proceed, the One is beyond subsistence,[14] beyond entity,[15] beyond act (I, 7, 1, 19–20; VI, 7, 17, 9–11), beyond life (V, 3, 16, 38).

Plotinus, in fact, affirms that the One is,[16] and denies that it is (VI, 7, 38, 1–4; VI, 8, 8, 14–15); affirms that it subsists,[17] and denies that it subsists (VI, 8, 10, 35–38; VI, 8, 11, 1–5); affirms that it is act (VI, 8, 20, 13–15), and denies that it is act (III, 8, 11, 7–10); affirms that it is free (VI, 8, 20, 17–19), and denies that it is free (VI, 8, 8, 9–12); affirms that it has life (V, 4, 2, 17–18), and denies that it has life (VI, 7, 17, 12–14). Plotinus is not contradicting himself. The One is or has all these, to the extent that neither they nor the being or having of them involves duality. When Plotinus denies an attribute of the One he does so to affirm the simplicity of the One; when he affirms an attribute he shows that the One, although simple, is not negative. Plotinus applies negative formulae to the One, not to deny positivity of it, but to deny duality. The One, which needs nothing, is by the same token deprived of nothing: it is the most sufficient, the least lacking (VI, 9, 6, 17–18). Thus positive formulae can be applied to the One, provided that they be qualified to remove the taint of duality: the One has quasi-subsistence, quasi-entity, quasi-life, which are identical with itself (VI, 8, 7, 49–54).

These considerations about the nature of the One furnish valuable preliminary notions of what production and knowledge can be for the One. If the One, which is perfectly simple, produces, it cannot be by any dissipation of itself, any going out from itself. If it knows, it cannot know in any way that would place it in apposition to itself and make it two. And yet, as it is not negative, if it produces it veritably produces, and if it knows it veritably knows.

THE ONE—POIESIS

According to the "incorrect" mode of speaking, the One makes itself. It, and its willing of itself, are one: in this sense it produced itself (VI, 8, 13; cf. VI, 8, 7, 52–54). More properly, it does not make itself subsist, and nothing else makes it subsist (VI, 8, 10, 36–38); its self-mastery is above will (VI, 8, 9, 44–45), since it is above any shadow of duality that self-mastery might connote (V, 3, 17, 14). The One is above necessity, that is, above any exterior constraint; it is what it ought to be, but it is so entirely through itself (VI, 8, 9).

The One, self-constituted, generates the Nous, but remains perfectly stable and unmoved in doing so. The One does not incline forward. It generates as the sun generates the light about it.[18]

Plotinus makes frequent use of the example of the generation of light by the sun to explain generation and production.[19] The point of comparison is twofold: the generation, or emission, involves no diminution of the source; the source is simultaneous with the generated and the emitted. These comparisons are possible because Plotinus apparently believed that the sun is not weakened by the emission of light, and that light takes no time to proceed from a source to an illuminable object (IV, 3, 10, 1–7).

The One has all power; indeed, it is the power of producing all things (V, 4, 2, 39–40). It is the master of this power precisely in the sense that it does not need the things that come after it. It does not need them at all: it is the same after generating them as before, in fact, their generation or non-generation is indifferent to it (V, 5, 12, 39–44).

"[The One], being perfect, by not seeking anything, or having anything, or needing anything, overflows as it were, and its superabundance makes another. . . ." (V, 2, 1, 7–9.) The One, being perfect, overflows *as it were*. It overflows as perfect; it overflows because it is perfect. Its overflowing is a *quasi* overflowing because it is and remains perfect: a *quasi* overflowing because in itself it is unaffected. It is and remains perfect precisely in the sense that it seeks nothing, has nothing, and needs nothing. The One produces all things by having no need of them. By being perfect—and it is perfect—it must produce. Or, more properly, it produces *simpliciter*—it just does produce:

And, so long as they remain, all beings give, from their own entity, around themselves and towards what is outside themselves, and from their present power, an hypostasis necessarily depending on them. This hypostasis is as it were the image of the archetype from which it is produced. Fire gives the heat which issues from it: and snow does not hold the cold solely within itself. Odoriferous things bear special witness to this. So long as they are, there proceeds something from them, about them, so that the nearest of things standing around partakes of it. Now everything which is already perfect generates. That which is always perfect generates always, and generates something eternal. (V, 1, 6, 30–39.)

What we must note here is the complete connection of perfection with generation. Everything that is already perfect generates, so that the One, which is always perfect, always generates. All beings generate so long as they remain (*menei*). Although a very general sense of *menei* in Plotinus is "stay immobile," and although this interpretation would strengthen the application to the One in this passage, it seems likely that here *menei* means rather "endure." Ficino renders it "perseverant." The conclusion is that that which is always perfect generates something eternal: the point seems to be the *enduring* of the generator.

The phrase "from their own entity" (*ek tês autôn ousias*) admits of two interpretations: that the generated is produced from the entity of the generator as from a material; that the generated is produced from the entity of the generator as from a source. What has been cited up to this point regarding generation by the One would indicate that the latter is the proper interpretation here. It is true that the examples which Plotinus uses, fire, snow, and odoriferous things, might suggest the former. But in another passage, in which he again compares the generation of the Nous by the One to the generation of heat by fire, he explains clearly the sense in which he wishes us to understand "from their own entity."

According to V, 4, 2, 27–39, the act *of* the entity is to be distinguished from the act *from* the entity. There is a heat *of* fire which is the same as fire itself, and a heat that derives *from* fire. When the fire, by remaining just what it is, exercises the heat within itself which is the same as itself, then the heat "towards the external" (*pros to hexô*) has already necessarily come to be.

The One, remaining in itself, in its own proper seat,[20] has its perfection in itself and exercises its own co-subsistent act, which is itself. The Nous necessarily takes its hypostasis *from* this intimate act of the One, and in doing so comes to being and entity. Thus the doctrine has been expressed with precision. The self-act of the One is and remains complete in itself; the Nous is the act *from* the self-contained self-act of the One as from an originative source. The act *from* the entity is necessary when the act *of* the entity is exercising itself.

In this same passage Plotinus says that the Nous "takes its

hypostasis," it "comes to being and to entity" (V, 4, 2, 37–39). In general, whatever is lower "comes towards" the higher to receive entity, form, or order.[21] This metaphor calls attention to the relative self-containedness of all higher principles, and to their indifference to the lower; it at least balances the metaphor of outpouring. It is as though one were to say that an artifact "comes towards" the artisan, in that it begins to measure up to his artistic *habitus* or "creative idea."

Plotinus' doctrine has been seen to be that, so long as they endure, all beings give, from their own entity *as an originative source,* an hypostasis necessarily dependent[22] on them. The dependent hypostasis is "around" the source (V, 1, 6, 31). This is not a spatial concept, but only a spatial metaphor: it is meant to convey the ontic contiguity of generator and generated. The dependent hypostasis is given "from the present power" (*ibid.,* line 32) of the generator, that is, from the generator's power, which is present. This phrase is an explicit expression of a notion central to Plotinus' doctrine of producing: productive, i.e., generative or poietic agents, act by their mere presence.

The dependent hypostasis is an image (*eikôn*) of the generator. This concept and kindred ones are applied in many places where Plotinus wishes to characterize the lower in relation to the higher. The Nous is the *eikôn* (V, 1, 7, 1), the *mimêma,* and the *eidôlon* (V, 4, 2, 26–27) of the One. Similarly, the soul is the *eikôn,* the *mimêma* (V, 8, 12, 16–17), and the *eidôlon* (V, 1, 7, 39) of the Nous. In general, each productive agent is the *mimêma* of its producers (III, 8, 7, 6–7). *Eikôn* means "image," and for Plotinus the primary sensuous analogate of the word is not image in the sense that a statue is an image, but image in the sense of an image in a mirror:

> But if someone says that it is not necessary that the image (*eikôn*) be connected closely with the archetype—for it happens that the image subsists when the archetype, from which the image arose, is absent, . . . First of all, if he is speaking of an image issuing from a painter, we do not say that the archetype has produced the image, but rather that the painter has, and it is not *his* image, even if someone were to portray himself. For the picture is not either the body of the painter, or the form (which

it imitates)—we ought to think that it is not the painter, but rather some certain disposition of colors that makes such an image. And this is not the making, in the primary sense, of an image (*eikôn*) and an appearance (*indalma*), such as in water and in mirrors and in shadows. In these cases the image takes its entity truly from what is before it and is born from this, and it does not happen that the generated exists, when it is cut off from the generator.   (VI, 4, 10, 1–15.)

To call the dependent hypostasis the image of the generator connotes, then, a complete dependence of the produced upon its producer, and a relative lack of reality of the lower with reference to the higher.[23]

In the generation of the Nous, the world of true being, by the One, all possible effects are realized. The One has an internal freedom, but its producing of Being and beings is necessary. "It was not fitting that the power [of the One] be arrested, as though circumscribed by jealousy, but it always advances, until all things, down to the last, come to the limit of their possibility . . ." (IV, 8, 6, 12–14); ". . . if something more could be generated from it, nothing would be for it an object of jealousy. Now, however, there is nothing to be generated, there is nothing which is not generated, since everything has been generated." (V, 5, 12, 44–47.)

This, then, is Plotinus' basic notion of production. When the producing agent does not go out of itself, and does not exert effort (V, 3, 12, 27–33), producing is at its best—not in spite of these conditions, but precisely because of them. In general, relatively perfect, relatively unchanging, relatively self-contained producing agents produce necessarily and eternally for the exact reason that they are perfect, unchanging, and self-contained. This notion of producing will be applied, in a diminished fashion, to the conception of nature as a productive agent.

THE ONE—KNOWLEDGE

Does the One have knowledge? Does it contemplate? Nature, soul, and Nous are contemplations; is the One in any sense a contemplation? Plotinus' first answer to these questions follows the general line of his negative doctrine of the One. Knowledge cannot be at-tributed to the One, just as subsistence, life, etc., cannot be attrib-uted to it, for to attribute anything to the One is to make it two. "Therefore do not add knowledge to the One, so as not to add another to it, and to make two, the knower and the Good." (III, 8, 11, 12–14.) The One does not need knowledge (V, 3, 12, 49–50; V, 6, 4, 1–2); the One does not have knowledge.

Not only would the ascription of knowledge to the One make the One dual, but knowledge in itself is not perfectly simple. Knowledge requires an object of knowledge, an entity. In the Nous, where knowledge exists at its highest, there is a *unity* be-tween knowledge and its object, but this unity is not the unquali-fied One (V, 6, 6, 22–28). No knower is absolutely simple, therefore the One cannot be a knower (cf. V, 3, 11, 26–31). Plotinus in fact devotes an entire treatise (V, 6) to showing, on this and on similar grounds, that the One does not know. In addition, he argues in many other places the impropriety and impossibility of the One's having knowledge.[24] Concentration upon such texts would lead us to believe that the question is closed, the answer settled for Plotinus. The One knows neither itself nor anything else (VI, 7, 39, 19–20).

And yet, to say that the One does not know itself does not, for Plotinus, mean that the One is ignorant of itself. Ignorance, like knowledge, implies a duality: in the case of ignorance, there is the object which is *not* known. The One neither knows nor is ignorant (VI, 9, 6, 42; cf. VI, 7, 37, 23–28); it is more properly beyond knowl-edge (V, 3, 12, 48–49; VI, 7, 40, 24–29).

The One does not know because a knower is never perfectly one; it does not know because knowledge implies a duality: per-haps Plotinus means that the One does not know *insofar as* knowl-edge implies duality. Knowledge in its proper sense is dual: but might there not be a quasi-knowledge in the One as there is quasi-hypostasis and quasi-life? Might there not be a cognitive state positively beyond knowledge, a state which would be simple and not dual?

According to a plausible interpretation of one passage, the One has, in place of knowledge, a self-contact:

Thus it is necessary that the knower take up different things, and that the known, being known, be varied: or there will not be knowledge of the known, but rather a touching, and as it were a contact only, not spoken and not known, a pre-knowing (*pronoousa*) when Nous has not yet been generated, and the toucher does not know. . . . Knowledge is, as it were, a finding by one who has sought. That which is altogether without difference [the One] itself remains towards itself, and seeks nothing about (*peri*) itself.   (V, 3, 10, 40–43; 49–51.)

It might be said that this text refers to the contact of the individual soul with the One. But the expression "before the Nous is generated" shows that Plotinus is dealing with the One in itself.[25]

When Plotinus is speaking "incorrectly," he brings together the two notions of the One's contact with itself and its being towards itself in a sentence that specifies the attitude towards itself as a making: "The One, as it were, made itself by an act of looking at itself. This act of looking at itself is, in a way, its being." (VI, 8, 16, 19–21.)

We do not stretch the meaning of this text to say that, in it, the One is called a *self-contemplation*, as Nous, as soul, as nature are, in their own fashions, self-contemplations. It should be noted that Plotinus does not scruple to speak here of the being or quasi-being of the One, as he speaks elsewhere of its ousia (entity, beingness) or quasi-ousia (VI, 8, 13, 5–10).

In these lines the One is said to look at itself, and a little further on in the same passage the One is called an eternal super-knowledge: "If, now, its [the One's] act does not become but is always, and is a kind of wakefulness which is not other than the one who is awake, being a wakefulness and an eternal super-knowledge (*hypernoêsis*), it will *be* in the way it is awake. The wakefulness is beyond being and Nous and intelligent life; the wakefulness is itself." (VI, 8, 16, 31–36.)

A wakefulness which is a *super*-knowledge, or a wakefulness which is *above* knowledge? It is true that the word *hypernoêsis* will bear either interpretation. But there are several indications in this same general context that Plotinus intends the positive sense, super-knowledge.

He has said a little above that "the most lovable in the One is, as it were, the Nous" (*ibid.*, line 15). The force of this becomes manifest when we realize that he can not be referring to the hypostasis, the Nous. The One is the Good, the good for the Nous-hypostasis as well as for everything else,[26] the supremely lovable. Here he says that the most lovable in this supremely lovable is, as it were, intelligence.

Ennead VI, 8, 18 echoes the same thought. There is in the One a sort of intelligence which is not the Nous. The One is the center; from it radiate being and Nous. Being and Nous, as they are poured forth from the One and depend on its intellectual nature, bear witness to the fact that there is knowledge in the One.

These passages occur in the contexts in which Plotinus is allowing himself a certain latitude in characterizing the One. But in V, 4, 2, with no apologies for speaking without rigor, he states unequivocally that the One has self-knowledge. After remarking that the Nous is multiple (as containing the multiplicity of the ideas and as being composed of the known and the knower), Plotinus goes on to say that the One is "not, so to speak, imperceptive, but everything of it is in it and with it [i.e., it is entirely self-contained]; it is entirely self-discerning; life is in it and all things are in it; and its self-knowledge is itself, a self-knowledge by a kind of synesthesis being in eternal stasis and in a knowledge otherwise than knowledge according to the Nous."[27]

Thus knowledge, which appears in a way in nature, more fully in soul, perfectly in the Nous, is not absent from the highest "nature," the One: the continuity of knowledge is not abruptly broken in the ascent from the Nous to the One.[28]

A knowledge which is a self-identity—this is not so alien to Plotinus' usual notion of knowledge as may first appear. On all levels the nisus of knowledge is towards identity: knowledge becomes truer as knower and known become more identical. In the Nous, he tells us, "the theoria must be the same as the contemplated, and the Intelligence the same as the intelligible. For, if they were not the same, there would not be truth. For the possessor would have an imprint of beings instead of the beings, wherefore there would not be truth." (V, 3, 5, 21–25.)

The next chapter will discuss the sense in which this identity of knower and known in the Nous is to be taken, in the face of the doctrine of the duality of the Nous. Important in the present context are the notions of true knowledge as an identity and of identity as the gauge of truth and of knowledge. Since identity is the ideal of knowledge, and duality only its condition, the self-identical synesthesis of the One can be a super-knowledge in a positive sense.

The primary instance of knowledge in Plotinus' universe is, therefore, the One's super-knowledge. The primary instance of generation is the One's generation of the Nous. Taken together, these are the primary analogue of nature's contemplative producing.

NOTES

1. III, 8, 9, 1–13. It is curious that Dean Inge should leave out the major premise when he reproduces this argument. (William Ralph Inge, *The Philosophy of Plotinus*, 3rd ed., London 1928, II, 108–109.) Essentially the same argument is found in V, 1, 5, 1–18.

It should be added that Plotinus very frequently works the doctrine of the One into the general system of his philosophy without formal proofs. (Cf. II, 9, 1; IV, 8, 5; V, 2, 1; V, 4, 1 and 2, etc.)

2. III, 8, 11, 7–10. The identity of the One and the Good is stated concisely in II, 9, 1, 5 – 6: "When we say the One, and when we say the Good, we must understand that we are speaking of one and the same nature."

3. Porphyry, *De Vita Plotini*, ed. Paul Henry and Hans-Rudolph Schwyzer in *Plotini Opera* (Paris and Brussels, 1951–), I, 1– 41, ch. 23, lines 15–18.

4. "Moreover, the Nous is other than the Good: for it is conformed to the Good (*agathoeidês*) by knowing it." (V, 6, 4, 6–7.)

5. "Hypostasis" is not, for Plotinus himself, a common designation of the One. I have been able to find only one place (VI, 8, 15, 30) where he calls the One in so many words "the first hypostasis." In VI, 8, 20, 11, he apparently alludes to the One as an hypostasis. He speaks of the One's "*having* hypostasis" (V, 6, 3, 11), of the "hypostasis *of* the Good" (VI, 8, 13, 43–44), of "*its* quasi-hypostasis" (VI, 8, 7, 47) (italics mine). It would seem that the designation of the One as an hypostasis in systematic accounts of Plotinus' philosophy is based on the title of V, 1, which treatise is an elementary outline of the doctrine of the One, the Nous, and the soul: "About the Three Hypostases Which Are Principles" (*peri tôn triôn archikôn hypostaseôn*). This title, however, like all the titles of Plotinus' treatises, is not Plotinus' own (Porphyry, ch. 4, lines 16–18). In speaking of the One, the Nous, and the soul in this treatise, Plotinus calls them "these three" (V, 1, 10, 5), or "the three natures" (V, 1, 8, 27).

6. V, 5, 6, 23–25. In VI, 9, 4, 11–12, Plotinus applies to the One a formula from the first hypothesis of Plato's *Parmenides*: "It can be neither said nor written." (*Parmenides* 142a)

7. I, 7, 1, 20–22 and *passim*: I, 8, 1–5; V, 1, 6, 50–53.

8. Cf. VI, 7, 41, 27–31: "Thus it [the Good] is not good for itself, but for the others. For they have need of it, but it has no need of itself. It would be absurd that it should have need of itself, for this would mean that it lacked itself." Cf. VI, 9, 6, 40–42.

9. *par' hautou*, VI, 8, 14, 42; *eph' hautou*, VI, 8, 11, 33; *eph´ heautou*, VI, 9, 6, 15.

10. *pros hauton kai es auton*, VI, 8, 17, 26; *pros hauto*, V, 3, 10, 51.

11. The One is "cause of itself" (*aition heautou*) VI, 8, 14, 42; "it made itself to subsist" (*Autos ara hypestêsen hauton*), VI, 8, 16, 30; "it makes itself" (*auto hauto poiei*), VI, 8, 7, 53; it "has made itself" (*auton pepoiêkenai hauton*), VI, 8, 13, 54 –55. The word "constitutes" itself has been used to render these phrases and to express a causality which is not precisely either efficient or final.

12. The Good is *hikanon heautô(i)* in I, 8, 2, 4–5. It is *hikanôtaton* in VI, 9, 6, 17.

13. I, 8, 2, 4–5; VI, 9, 6, 18; *ibid.*, lines 24–26.

14. *epekeina ara ontos*, V, 5, 6, 11; *pro hypostaseôs*, VI, 8, 10, 37.

15. In his doctrine of the One-Good, Plotinus makes frequent use of Plato's phrase (*Rep.* VI, 509b9) *epekeina ousias*, the Good is beyond entity. *Vide:* V, 1, 8, 8 (where he quotes Plato directly and with approval); V, 4, 1, 9–10; VI, 7, 40, 26; VI, 9, 11, 42, etc.

16. With regard to the Good, "allow it to be" (*eiase to estin*), V, 5, 13, 12–13. "If anyone says that the Good is not (*mê eiêai*), there would be no evil" (VI, 7, 23, 15–16). Cf. V, 3, 10, 48– 49; VI, 7, 23, 9–10; VI, 8, 16, 19–21.

17. VI, 8, 11, 33; cf. VI, 8, 13, 50–52, where again Plotinus says that the One subsists, but has noted immediately before (*ibid.*, lines 47–50) that he is not speaking rigorously.

18. "It is necessary that [the One] be unmoved, if there is to be a second after it: it makes the latter to subsist (*hypostênai auto*) without inclining forward, or willing or being moved in any way. How, then? And how ought we to think of the One which is stable? An illumination from it, from the immobile One, as the light which is about the light of the sun—generated from it, which remains eternally." (V, 1, 6, 25–30.)

19. E.g., I, 7, 1, 24–28; cf. Plato, *Rep.* VI, 508e–509a; V, 3, 9, 15–20.

20. *en tô(i) oikeiô(i) êthei,* V, 4, 2, 22. This phrase, repeated in line 35, is taken from Plato, *Timaeus,* 42e, where it refers to the Demiurge *after* the production of the visible cosmos. It could also be rendered "remaining in its proper custom or character," but there seems to be a strong echo of the radical meaning of *ethôs.*

21. E.g., body comes to soul rather than soul to body (VI, 4, 12, 33–41); in so doing body comes to real being and the world of life (*ibid.,* lines 41–46). The same doctrine is expressed in V, 4, 16, 7–13. According to III, 4, 1, 8–9, all generation takes place in two steps: the generator produces a generated which is formless and relatively indeterminate; the generated *turns back to* the generator and in so doing becomes formed and determinate. *Vide infra,* pp. 61–62; 137–138.

22. If *anangkaian* is to be construed as modifying *hypostasin*—and this seems the only possibility, despite its position in the sentence—then Plotinus is saying that the generated hypostasis is necessary and dependent, therefore, since this is probably an hendiadys, *necessarily* dependent. Ficino has: "Jam vero res omnes . . . *necessarium* circa se foras *naturam* producunt ab ipsis pendentem . . ."; but Bréhier, apparently taking *anangkaian* as a substantive and a synecdochical accusative, has: "Tous les êtres d'ailleurs, . . . produisent nécessairement autour d'eux . . . une réalité qui . . . dépend de leur pouvoir actuel . . ." (italics mine).

23. "Reality" is not a Plotinian technical term. I intend it here and elsewhere in a semi-popular sense, to mean that which is existent, not fictitious, not imaginary, not merely mental or ideal. I believe that Plotinus means everything from the One to matter to be a "reality" in this sense. "Reality" would not be equivalent to "being," which word Plotinus uses technically in the classic Greek philosophic sense of that which is eternal, changeless, limited, internally one (cf. e.g., VI, 5, 2, 9–16). Plato's forms are, precisely in this sense, beings. The Nous is the realm of being; the One is above being; the sensible world is below being; matter is non-being. But they are all "real." Reality, however, admits of degrees: the One is the most real; matter is the least real. For a development of the notion of degrees of reality, *vide infra,* pp.102–112.

24. E.g., III, 8, 11; III, 9, 9; V, 3, 11 and 12; VI, 7, 37– 41.

25. Plotinus also designates the pre-knowing contact of the One with itself as a "thrust": "Nothing else is present to the One, but there will be a certain simple thrust (epibolê) in it towards itself." (VI, 7, 38, 25–26). Further, it is this thrust towards itself (ibid., ch. 39, 1–2). Epiballein can carry the meaning "attend to, think on," so it is possible that in this Plotinus is speaking already of a quasi-knowledge in the One. Ficino translates epibolê "intuitus"; Bréhier, "intuition." If epibolê has this meaning, we have an indication of cognition by the One in the midst of a long development (VI, 7, 37– 41) of the argument that the One does not know.

26. Cf. III, 8, 11, 7–25. "The Nous has need of the Good [the One], but the Good has no need of the Nous" (lines 14–15).

27. V, 4, 2, 16–20. "Synesthesis" transliterates synaisthêsei. The alternate reading syn aisthêsei has considerable manuscript authority (Henry, app. crit. ad V, 4, 2, 18). Synaisthêsei conveys the notion of self-perception, or better, self-contained perception; syn aisthêsei would mean merely "with perception." Ficino double-translates: "atque animadversio sui ipsummet exsistit, tanquam cum quodam sensu suique consensu," which suggests either that he knew of both readings and did not wish to choose, or that he had before him a text which gave both readings. The latter case suggests that a copyist had not been able to choose.

28. Inge (II, 114) appears to agree that Plotinus' One cannot be said without qualification to be unknowing. He states: "It [the One] has a 'true noêsis,' different from that of nous," and cites in a footnote III, 8, 10, and V, 4, 2, as sources. Neither the phrase nor the doctrine occurs in III, 8, 10, which treats, in its concluding sentences, not of the One's "self-knowledge," but of a "knowledge" of, or better, a "thrust" to the One by the individual soul. The phrase, without the word "true," does occur in V, 4, 2, 19–20.

In further support of this thesis, Inge quotes without reference the statement that the One "abides in a state of 'wakefulness (egrêgorsis) beyond Being.'" The reference should be to VI, 8, 16, 34–35 (vide supra, p. 32–33).

He says also that, for Plotinus, the One "has 'self-discernment' (diakritikon heautou), which implies a sort of self-consciousness," and the reference reads: "6, 7, 16 and 5, 1, 7. He [the One] has *hoion synaisthêsin tês dynameôs hoti dynatai ousian.* He [Plotinus] even says *tê(i) epistrophê(i) pros hauto heôra hê de horasis hautê nous.*" This reference is unfortunate. The expression *diakritikon heautou* does not occur in either of the passages cited, but rather in V, 4, 2, 17. *Hoion synaisthêsin,* etc., is found in V, 1, 7, 12–13, where the context clearly shows that the possessor of this is not meant to be the One, but rather the Nous. *Tê(i) epistrophê(i),* etc., is V, 1, 7, 5–6; the reference is not to the interior self-knowledge of the One, but to the One's generating of the Nous, as is clear from the words immediately preceding: *all´ ou nous ekeino. Pôs oun noun genna(i); Ê hoti tê(i) epistrophê(i),* etc.

The general theme of both V, 1, 7 and VI, 7, 16 is, in fact, the generation of the Nous by the One. Inge appears to have mistaken expressions Plotinus uses in this connection for affirmations of the existence of a Nous, or of knowledge, within the One.

Pistorius, in support of his thesis that the One has "no thought," quotes a few familiar passages in which Plotinus says that the One has no knowledge, but fails to discuss any passage which could be taken to mean that the One does have knowledge. He sees that the chapter to which Inge makes reference, VI, 7, 16, is not concerned with the One's self-knowledge, but he does not recognize that the phrase *diakritikon heautou* does not, in point of fact, come from this chapter. (Philippus Villiers Pistorius, *Plotinus and Neoplatonism,* Cambridge, England, 1952, pp. 10–11.)

3

CAUSED BY the One, the Nous, the second hypostasis, the knower-known (V, 3, 5, 26–29), the knowers-knowns (V, 9, 8, 1–7; VI, 7, 8, 27–29), is the one-many (V, 1, 8, 23–27). The One is above being; the Nous is identical with true being.[1] The One generates the Nous; the Nous in turn generates the soul (V, 2, 1, 14–18) and, apparently with soul as intermediary (V, 1, 3, 4–10), the visible cosmos (III, 2, 2, 1–2; V, 9, 9, 3–14). The One has super-knowledge; the Nous is the first instance of knowledge specifically so-called, and of contemplation.

THE NOUS—POIESIS

In giving a certain something of itself[2] to, or more properly, to-wards matter, Nous worked, wrought (*ergazesthai*) all things while remaining at rest (III, 2, 2, 15–16). "The power of producing through itself belongs to something which is not in all respects perfect: such a thing produces and is moved, according to the measure of its imperfection. But altogether blessed beings stand in themselves and are as they are; it is not safe for them to be busy about many things (*polupragmonein*), for that would mean to move out of themselves. But the Nous is so blessed that in not making it *works*, and in remaining self-contained it *makes*, great things." (III, 2, 1, 38–45.)

The power of production is thus attributed to Nous, but only in a sense that does not compromise its remaining by itself, its stasis with reference to its producing. It does not move in producing. It does not have the power of producing through itself in any sense that would connote movement or involvement: *polupragmonein*, involvement with many things, a word which Ficino renders as "negotiari," cannot be applied to Nous. There is a paradox even in the application of the notion of making or producing: Plotinus is purifying the verb *poiein*, "to make," for the purposes of his own philosophy. The Nous produces simply by being and remaining what it is. This notion of production will function in the description of the poiesis appropriate to soul and nature—but with modifications.

The intelligibles in the Nous do not subsist for the sake of producing: this is shown by the fact that they are prior to sensible things (VI, 7, 8, 5–12). By a slight inference, Plotinus can be understood to mean that the Nous is not solely or primarily a productive power. The Nous, then, does not subsist for the sake of producing; yet, if the intelligibles subsist, the sensibles follow from a necessity inherent in the intelligibles (*ibid.*, lines 12–13), that is, the Nous produces necessarily. As Plotinus puts it in III, 2, 2:

> [The visible cosmos] was born, not by any reasoning about the necessity (*dein*) of its generation, but by a necessity (*anankê(i)*) of the second nature [the Nous]: for the Nous was not such that it should be the last of beings. For it is the first, having much power, indeed all power; and it has this power to produce another without seeking to produce. If it sought, it would already not have this power from itself, from its own entity; but it would be like an artisan who does not have the power of production from himself, but by acquisition, having acquired it from learning. (Lines 8–15.)

In learning his art, and thereby acquiring the power of producing, the artisan shows that he does not have this power from himself or from his own entity. Since the power is not *his* in this full sense, he must, if he is to produce at all, *seek* to produce. The Nous does not seek to produce; it has its productive power from itself, it produces by a necessity inherent in it. Nor does the Nous reason about the production of the sensible world. Reasoning is the concomitant of seeking and learning. The disposition of the world according to Nous is more intelligent than a hypothetical disposition according to reasoning.[3] There is no seeking or reasoning. The intelligible world, archetype of the sensible world, subsists, and since there is nothing to hinder its action, it is necessary that the Nous order the sensible world, and that the sensible world be ordered by the Nous (V, 9, 9, 8–14).

The Nous produces by being and remaining exactly itself; it is not primarily a productive power, yet it produces necessarily. There is a temptation to term such a mode of production "automatic." This, however, is not Plotinus' term. He explicitly denies that the producing of the sensible world by the Nous is "automatic" simply because, in this producing, the Nous, intelligence—being prior not chronologically but in the sense of ontic originative source, as an intelligent-intelligible archetype and paradigm—brings it about that Nous is present in all things. The inference is that, for Plotinus, "automatic" would denote non-intelligent producing,[4] whereas producing by the Nous is at once intelligent and necessary (III, 2, 1).

In the doctrine of the Nous, then, "making" means a kind of producing to which the subsistence of the producer is ontically prior, one in which the producer is not in any way moved; a producing which is intelligent, but not according to a discursion or deliberation; a producing which is, therefore, necessary. These qualities appertain, by a principle of diminution which will be illustrated as its application is called for, to producing by soul and by nature as well.

THE NOUS—KNOWLEDGE AND CONTEMPLATION

The Nous, like the One, produces by being itself. In the Nous's case, however, to be itself is to be intellective, to be the intellectual knower.

In the Nous, contemplation is intellectual knowledge. The Nous possesses, or rather is, truth, because in it there is an identity of knower, knowing, and thing known, of contemplator, contemplation, and object of contemplation. These identifications are established in V, 3, 5, and III, 8, 8. According to the former, "... the contemplation (*tên theôrian*) must be the same as the thing contemplated (*tô(i) theôretô(i)*), and the Nous the same as the thing known *(tô(i) noêtô(i))*—for indeed, if it is not the same, there will be no truth." (V, 3, 5, 21–25.) A few lines further on Plotinus establishes the identity of knowing (*noêsis*) and the thing known (*ibid.*, line 43). According to III, 8, 8, 1–10:

> In the ascent of theoria from nature to soul and from soul to Nous, the theoriai become ever more intimate to, and united with, the contemplators. In the excellent soul the things known (*tôn egnôsmenôn*) are moving towards [an identification with] the soul as a subject, because they are aspiring to intelligence. In the Nous both are one, not by intimacy, as with the best soul, but by entity, and *to be* and *to know* are the same.[5] There is not still a difference—if there were, there would be something prior in which there was no difference. Therefore it is necessary that the Nous be both, as really one.

In III, 8, 8, Plotinus makes another identification, to which he alludes only in passing in V, 3, 5. Life and knowledge are co-ordinate. The Nous, which is its own knowledge, its own theoria, is the first life, living through itself (*autozôn*):

> This is a living theoria, not a theorema (*theôrêma*), that is, not a theorema in another. For the theorema which is in another is a certain living thing, not self-living. If, then, a certain theorema and noema (*noêma*) is to live, it must be self-life, not vegetative, or sensitive, or the other kinds of soul-life. For these other lives are also, in a way, knowledges: but the one is vegetative knowledge (*phutikê noêsis* [perhaps "naturely knowledge"]), the other sensitive, the last soul-knowledge. How are they knowledges? Because they are logoi. And every life is a certain knowledge, but one is more obscure than the other, just as the kinds of life are. The clearest knowledge is itself the first life, one with the first Nous. . . . For every life is of this kind and is a knowledge . . . . But this is to be noted, that again in passing our lecture [or perhaps "reason"] shows that all things are theoriai.
>
> (III, 8, 8, 11–26.)

The differences among knowledges are primarily differences on the scale of clarity and obscurity. In another place, Plotinus calls sensations obscure knowledges, and the knowledges in the Nous, clear sensations (VI, 7, 7, 30–31). Naturely (vegetative) knowledge, nature's theoria, is more obscure even than sensation-knowledge, but is still, in a way, knowledge.

To continue the presentation of III, 8: "If now the truest life is life in knowledge (*noêsei*),[6] if the truest life is the same as the truest knowledge, the truest knowledge lives, theoria and such a theorema are living things and life, and the two are one." (III, 8, 8, 26–30.) There is, then, a scale of knowledge and truth which is the same as the scale of life. The clearer knowledges, the clearer lives, are the truer knowledges and the truer lives. The clearest and truest is the Nous itself.[7]

The mention of theorema in these passages is worthy of attention. From its etymology, theorema could mean object of contemplation, or work of contemplation.[8] (We recall that for Plotinus contemplation has a work, a product.) Similarly, the co-ordinate noema could mean either work of knowledge or object of knowledge. The close parallel between this passage and V, 3, 5 (*vide supra*, p. 42–43) seems to indicate that the Nous's theorema is the same as the *theôrêton* and *noêton* mentioned there, and so should be taken as "object of knowledge." It is probably the same as the *egnôsmena* mentioned on page 43 which are surely objects of knowledge. Further, it seems doubtful that Plotinus considers that the Nous has an internal product of knowledge. His doctrine in many places is that, in the Nous, being is prior to the knower.[9]

The point here, however, is that Plotinus is speaking of the Nous's *internal* theorema. This can be shown from the text. The theoria which is Nous is said to be a living theoria, not a theorema such as would be in another. But that is not to say that it is not a theorema at all, or that all theoremata are in another, for the immediately following sentence shows that it is a self-living theorema. Plotinus is, then, contrasting theorema in another with self-living theorema.

What is the bearing of this contrast? The self-living theorema, in the Nous and identical with the Nous, is identical with theoria. Nature-life, animal-life, etc., are not self-living theoremata. This suggests, but does not say in so many words, that in the cases of nature and soul, theorema is not identical with theoria. In these cases, then, there would be a theorema in another. But this passage leaves the meaning of *in another* indefinite. *In another* in the sense of being in another subject, or *in another* in the sense of being not perfectly united to the subject in which it is?

It is said that in the ascent of theoria the theoriai become ever more closely united to the contemplators—this, then, would be a case of an increasing internal union; but it is not said specifically that the theoriai become more closely united to the theoremata— and if this were the case the question would still be open.

Plotinus has said that theorema in another is a certain living thing, but that if theorema is to live, it must be self-life, not nature-life or soul-life. This seems to mean that if theorema is to live *in the fullest sense of the word*, to live with the first life, it must be self-life. It is not said that the other kinds of life are other kinds of theoremata or noemata, but only that they are other knowledges, other kinds of theoriai. The other knowledges are identified with the other lives; the other theoremata are not; and their connection with the other lives is left indefinite.

Therefore in III, 8, 8, Plotinus establishes the identity of theoria and a certain type of theorema in the case of the Nous. He offers a hint of a dissociation of theoria and theorema in cases other than that of the Nous, but he furnishes no sure indication of whether this dissociation is internal, or external, or both, or of what its precise nature may be.

We have seen that there is an ordering of lives and knowledges according to increasing clarity from nature to Nous; there is an ascent of contemplation from nature to Nous. The theoria of the wise soul aims towards, and approximates, the theoria of the Nous.

Plotinus' guiding principle here may be that notion of continuity and difference which he expresses in *Ennead* V. The things that proceed from the One are, as it were, all along one living line. Each one is a part of this line, holding its own proper place—and the places are arranged according to anteriority and posteriority, so that the latter places are "worse." But each part is continuous with the whole line, so that the second part does not lose the first part, but receives and passes on the influence of the first part, etc. In the "descent" each is left in its own proper place; in the "return" the generated, that which took the worse place, can become the same as that on which it "draws" so long as it pursues this (V, 2, 2, 1–4; 27–30).

The first ten lines of III, 8, 8, given above, appear to echo this doctrine. As the excellent soul rises towards Nous, its theoria becomes ever more intimate to itself as contemplator—yet in the Nous theoria and contemplator are the same, not by intimacy, but by entity. This suggests that soul and Nous are on the same line, that soul has its proper place and keeps its proper place. It keeps its proper place, however, only to the extent that it does not, in its pursuit of Nous, become that which it draws upon.

A closer analysis indicates, however, that the notion of an ordering of lives, knowledges, and theoriai according to clarity and obscurity, such as has been found in III, 8, 8, may be connected with a notion of continuity, but is not equivalent to it. There is no mention of a persistence of the higher in the lower, or even of an influence of the higher upon the lower. The grades of life-knowledge could be more distinct than is envisaged in the continuity passage, but the mention of them has been prefaced by the allusion to the progress of the excellent soul. It seems best, then, to suppose that the passage is not to be taken merely as an account of statically distinct grades of life-knowledge, but at least to imply their dynamic relations with one another.

The Nous, then, represents an ideal of contemplation of which other principles fall short and towards which they strive: a contemplation entitatively united with the contemplator and with a self-living theorema. This is the world of true being.

NOTES

1. V, 9, 3, 1–4; cf. III, 6, 6, 16–17; V, 3, 5, 26–29.

2. This "something of itself" is logos. *Vide infra*, pp. 74 ff.

3. "Moreover, the ordering is in accordance with Nous in this way, as to be without discursive reasoning (*hôs aneu logismou einai*), yet it is such that it is remarkable that, if a man were able to make use of the best in the line of discursive reasoning, reasoning would not find how to do otherwise than after the fashion which is evident even in individual natures when things take place towards the ever more knowable rather than according to an ordering by discursive reasoning." (III, 2, 14, 1–6.)

Bréhier translates *hôs aneu logismou einai* by "sans provenir d'un dessein réfléchi." Ficino has "absque rationis discursione." "Réfléchi" could be misleading here. Bréhier tries to tie his rendering of *logismos* as "reflection" to *Timaeus*, 34a, where the motion of the Demiurge is said to be circular because in returning upon itself it suits the sort of intelligence proper to the Demiurge, i.e., a reflective intelligence. Here, however, the term reflection might translate an aspect of *logismos*, if we take care to mean by it not self-knowledge, which the Nous surely has, but deliberation, of which the Nous has no need. The "order in accordance with Nous" is beyond deliberation or rational construction because the Nous is never in a state of indecision, of having to say to itself, "Well, now, let me reflect and see what is best." The ideas are within it and it is in immediate possession of them.

4. III, 2, 1, 1–5: Plotinus here links the automatic or spontaneous with chance, *tô(i) automatô(i) kai tychê(i)*. This is traditional; cf. Aristotle *Phys.* II, 4–6, especially the distinction between them in 6, 197a36–b18. The spontaneous or automatic is also the non-intelligent for Aristotle, and this in the radical, substantial sense. Something can happen by chance to an intelligent being that could have intended it but did not; but if it happens to a being which by nature is non-intelligent, then it is spontaneous. Perhaps Plotinus here, as Aristotle in *Phys.* II, 4, 196a25, has in mind Democritus who ascribed "this heavenly sphere and all the worlds to spontaneity."

5. . . . *tauton to einai kai to noein einai*, a variant of Parmenides fr. 3, *to gar auto noein estin te kai einai*. It is probable that for Parmenides himself

this did not mean an identification of being and knowing, but rather that that which is and that which is known are one and the same.

6. Does Plotinus mean that the truest life is life *in* knowledge, life *through* knowledge, or life *according to* knowledge? The expression *noêsei zôê*, with no preposition before *noêsei*, is indefinite.

7. Cf. the identification in the Nous of *noein, zôê,* and *to einai* in V, 6, 6, 20–23. In general Plotinus' association of knowing, the truest life, and true being in the Nous recalls Plato's *Sophist,* 248e–249a: "And by the god, are we to be persuaded easily that, in truth, movement and life and soul and wisdom (*phronêsin*) are not present with perfect being, that it neither lives nor knows . . . ?"

8. For a discussion of these two meanings of theorema in Plotinus' doctrine of contemplation, *vide infra,* pp. 68 ff.

9. "Since being (*to on*) is first, it is necessary to take being first, then Nous. . . . Nous is the second, for it is the act of being (*ousias*)." (VI, 6, 8, 17–20.) "For if Nous were known before being, it would be necessary to say that the Nous by acting and knowing perfected and generated the beings: but since it is necessary to know being before the Nous, it is necessary to place the beings as lying in the knower (*tô(i) noounti*). The actuality and the knowledge is in the beings, as the act of fire is upon the fire, so that they will have their act, the Nous which is one of them." (V, 9, 8, 8–15.) The doctrine of a priority of being to the knower finds expression also in VI, 6, 6, 5–10; V, 9, 7, 16–17.

Two other passages, however, appear to compromise the doctrine of the priority of being. In VI, 7, 13, 28–29 we read that "there would not be beings if the Nous did not act." This might be interpreted in the sense above, that Nous or knowing is the actuality of being. But in V, 1, 7, 27–32, Plotinus says, "Of such a race is this Nous: it is worthy [to be called] the most pure Nous, being born not from any other source than from the first principle. Already generated, it generates together with it all beings (*ta onta panta*), all the beauty of the ideas, all the intelligible gods. Full of the beings which it has generated, it swallows them up in a way, retaining them in itself and preventing them from falling into matter."

4

IN PLOTINUS' world, the level below Nous is the domain of soul. Soul is the intermediary between the Nous and the sensible universe—an intermediary which, incidentally, seems endangered by the doctrine of the direct presence of matter to Nous. Nature is the lower part of the World Soul. The higher part is above nature, and so exhibits a prior, and better, instance of poiesis and contemplation.

SOUL AND NOUS

Pure soul, the highest part of soul, is said to be in the intelligible world.[1] Now the intelligible world, the realm of real being, is the Nous, and thus a difficulty is presented at once: How can the soul be a distinct hypostasis if it, or any part of it, is "in" another hypostasis? A possible answer would be that Plotinus uses the word "in" here in a special sense: a principle is said to be "in" that on which it depends, thus the body is "in" the soul (IV, 3, 9, 34–42). There is perhaps a suggestion of this meaning here, but the presence of the soul in the Nous seems to have the stronger significance of the presence of *a* real being in the *world* of real being. But the latter interpretation would mean a blurring of the distinction between the two hypostases, Nous and soul, for soul, as a being or beings within Being, would be as closely identified with Nous as any real being in the Nous. The proper meaning of the soul's being "in" the Nous, is, perhaps, that Nous is the super-reality of soul: Nous and soul are distinct hypostases, but not distinct existents.

In fact, the soul is generally spoken of as inferior to the Nous, and the expressions are various. The soul is not full, but falls short of that which is before it" (III, 8, 6, 26). The soul is the *eikôn* (V, 1, 3, 7) of the Nous, its *eidôlon*, its light, its dependent-trace (V, 1, 7, 39–43).

In one passage the Nous is the guarantor of the soul: the soul would not be eternal of itself without Nous, because everything in the cosmos is in matter and in body—thus, if the soul did not have Nous above it, "man" and all logoi would be neither eternal nor self-identical.[2] The soul is taken here as something in the cosmos, for it is said that "everything in the cosmos is in matter and in body" and *therefore* the soul would not be of itself eternal or self-identical. Apparently, even though the soul never unites with matter, or matter with it, nevertheless its contiguity to matter would preclude its eternality and self-identity were not the Nous above it, sustaining it.

While the soul is real being, it is also described as "from" real being in several striking formulae: "An animal comes to be. It has present to it a soul *from being,* according to which it depends upon all being; the body also is present . . ." (VI, 4, 15, 8–10). The soul is a principle from the intelligible world, co-present with a body when an animal comes to be. Again, the soul is called the act *from* entity (V, 2, 1, 16). The soul is the emissary from the Nous, the vehicle, as we shall see later, of the logoi (the principles of intellectuality), which effect the presence of Nous in all things, even in the things of nature, formed as they are by this lower part of the World Soul.

SOUL AND SOULS

Soul is not properly *in* body; rather, soul as the superior reality *contains* the sensible universe: i.e., the sensible universe is in soul.[3] Soul *in itself* is one and many, that is, its multiplicity is not consequent upon body or extension, but precedes bodies. Originally, the many souls are many, and are all in act in the one soul, but they are "particular without being particular" because their act is not directed to a particular body (VI, 4, 4, 36–40; VI, 4, 16, 33). The intelligences or knowers in the Nous, although they can be spoken of in the plural, are closely united. In the soul, the unity is more relaxed. The one soul suffices for each and all, because it contains all souls. It is one principle of life which has an infinity of lives (V, 4, 14, 1–9).

The soul as *one*, called "all soul" or "soul-entire," contains both individual souls and the World Soul as its quasi-parts (IV, 3, 8, 1–9). The World Soul is called the Soul of the All, that is, the soul of the sensible all, the sensible universe, and thus distinction must be made between "all soul" ("soul-entire") and the Soul of the All (World Soul).[4] An individual human soul is made up of two parts (II, 1, 5; IV, 3, 27) and sometimes three (II, 9, 2, 4–10). The description of nature as the lower part of the World Soul indicates that the World Soul has higher and lower parts. Thus Plotinus' texts indicate certain distinctions within this one and many, but often they must not be taken as hard and fast. Plotinus reiterates that all souls are one.[5] In some contexts the distinction between all-soul and the World Soul (Soul of the All) seems not to matter, and is consequently blurred—although in other contexts it is necessary to maintain it.[6] Furthermore, any soul is in some sort of continuity with soul-entire, and the human soul especially is capable of realizing its full articulation with soul-entire. The realm of soul is not precisely stratified or divided.

Let us try an interpretive device of limited value: recasting Plotinus' doctrine of the soul in Aristotelian terms. Is Plotinus saying that "soul" is a universal, applying to the life principles of diverse beings? No, the soul is one hypostasis, one entity. The necessarily inaccurate expression of his thought in this language would be that the soul is both a subsistent universal and the totality of beings to which this universal applies.

"Soul-entire" thus means at once subsistent soul quality (and therefore the highest, best soul), and all souls insofar as they are souls. It both includes and is superior to the "other" souls. Plotinus' own comparison is to genus and species: "The souls also must be many and one, and from the one soul there must be the many, which are different, as from one genus there are many species . . ." (IV, 8, 3, 10–12).

THE ROLE OF SOUL IN THE SENSIBLE WORLD

Plotinus inherited from Plato two notions of the role of soul in the sensible world. The one, to be identified generally with the doctrine of the *Phaedrus*, if taken literally would mean that the human soul, at least, has fallen culpably from a pre-existent state, and that its presence to the body is, for it, a violent condition (cf. *Phaedrus*, 246–248). The other, the doctrine of the *Timaeus*, makes the soul out to be an in-between reality, naturally fitted to govern the body (cf. *Timaeus*, 34a–35b; 41d–42e). Plotinus makes a serious effort to accommodate these two doctrines to each other. He tells us that the World Soul is not fallen. If it were fallen, it would have forgotten the intelligibles; had it done this, it could not have fashioned the world (II, 9, 4, 1–9). With regard to the individual souls the question is more complex. Already in Plato the notion of a "fall" is probably not to be understood as part of the *pre-history* of the individual soul, but as a mythical expression of its present state. *Now* the soul is out of relation to its own present higher self because of its present relationship to the body.

This is the way Plotinus interprets Plato here. Now, if we grant that Plato is speaking of a present relationship of the individual soul to the body, does the fall consist in the mere presence of the soul to the body, or in a "moral" turning by which the soul loses itself in the desires of the body? Plotinus makes a serious effort to distinguish between these two senses of "fall," and to say that the governance of the body can be effected without a moral turning to the body. This effort, however, is not consistently successful. In some places the soul seems to have (or to be) fallen off culpably from a better state, but this fall is represented as necessary for the good of the whole, or at least as redounding to the good of the body. In other places the fall is again culpable, but unavoidable in view of the necessary role the soul must play in the cosmic order.

Supposing that the fall is not a "moral" turning from the better to the worse, is it still a falling off from a better state? Plotinus seems to indicate in several places that it is. It would be hard for a Platonist to deny that soul, at least the human soul, is itself better without the body. Yet the World Soul is eternally governing its body, its body is eternally in it, and nevertheless it is eternally blessed. The difficulties remain.

Undoubtedly one reason for proposing parts of the soul is the effort to solve these problems. A higher part can be present with the Nous, a lower part involved with matter. But again, is it of the nature of soul to have these parts? Does the "projection" of a lower part involve a falling off, either in an ontic or in a moral sense? Is the soul, then, eternally "fallen," and if so, does this mean any more than that it is an inferior grade of being?

Probably the reason such questions can be raised is that in Plotinus' philosophy there is always a tendency to present lower grades of being as ontic and/or moral descents from higher grades: quite possibly this mode of presentation should be taken as metaphorical. Or, at the least, it can be said that there is a confusion in his thought between the "static" notion of the lower as worse than the higher and the "dynamic" notion of the lower as a worsening of the higher.

A detailed development in IV, 8, 1–5 shows Plotinus' strongest effort to establish the soul at its proper level and to show that it can rule the body without contamination.[7] In an historical introduction, Plotinus alludes to the apparent divergence between the doctrine of the *Phaedrus* and that of the *Timaeus* (IV, 8, 1, 23–50). Yet the difficulties *seem* to be resolved almost at once. The World Soul can govern the universe without contamination (IV, 8, 2, 15–33). Moreover, even "our soul, if it is united to this perfect soul, itself possesses perfection. It also 'traverses the heavens and governs the cosmos.' When it does not depart [from there] to nonbeing, to be the soul of bodies or of a particular body, then it also, as governing with the Soul of the All, easily governs the All, as[8] it is not evil in any way whatever for soul to present to body the power of well-being and of being, because not every providence for the worse takes away from the provider its remaining in the best."[9]

This seems clear enough. Plotinus might reasonably be taken to mean that even a human soul can perform its legitimate function with regard to a human body without fall, fault, or contamination. The immediate application of the passage, however, is to the souls of the stars, the souls which, according to the *Phaedrus*, did not descend. *These* are not moved from their blessed contemplation by the care of their bodies (IV, 8, 2, 51–54).

Plotinus will "now" speak of the human soul, as though he had not mentioned it previously. Apparently "our" soul is not precisely the same as the human soul. He does not say that the *human* soul can rule its body without contamination; he concedes that for the human soul the body is a prison and a tomb. But the blessed souls, i.e., the souls of the stars, can rule their bodies without contamination "because of the different reasons of the descent" (IV, 8, 3, 1–6). This could hardly apply to different reasons for the descents of different human souls; that would not touch the problem. It might mean different reasons for the descent of the souls of the stars on the one hand and of human souls on the other, if Plotinus would say that the souls of the stars "descend" in any sense from the Soul of the All.

The explanation which immediately follows recapitulates the doctrine of the Nous, the one-many, and the soul, the one-and-many (IV, 8, 3, 6–20). Then a highly important passage, by differentiating anew soul from Nous, shows that soul has its own proper function, and is necessary:

> The work of the more reasonable soul is to know intellectually, but not alone to know intellectually: in what respect would it differ from Nous? The soul, adding to its intellectuality something else, according to which it will have its proper hypostasis, did not remain Nous; but it too has a work, if indeed everything, whatever being it may be, has its proper work. Looking towards that which is before it, it knows intellectually; looking into itself it keeps itself; looking towards that which is after it, it orders and governs and rules this: so that it was not possible for all to stand in the intelligible, when another was able to come to be in the sequence, and to be worse, but necessary, as indeed that before it was necessary.   (IV, 8, 3, 21–31.)

"The soul . . . did not remain Nous"—neither was it possible "for all to stand in the intelligible." Here is the theme of a declination from the higher, intimately connected, however, with a clear statement that the soul has its own proper hypostasis, and performs its own work. Its "work" is described as a looking, i.e., a contemplating, indeed as a threefold looking characteristic of its intermediate state. And, however much the soul may be a declination from the Nous, it is still necessary; that is, even though soul is "worse" than Nous, there must be soul, at its own proper level. This form of the argument, manifesting the necessity for soul, is resumed by Plotinus in chapter 5 of this treatise.

Can the particular soul perform its work as soul without

contamination from the body? The argument of Plotinus' chapter 4 involves a difficult mingling of themes, and its import is not clear. If, or when, souls remain in the intelligible with soul-entire, they are unharmed and "administer with it," like kings who live with the pantocrator and do not depart from his palace. *Then* all souls are together in one place (IV, 8, 4, 5–10). These expressions would seem to imply a possible state of things in which there would be a joint administration of the world by the souls. But no details are given of this co-administration. Could particular souls have the particular care of individual bodies while remaining in the intelligible with soul-entire? Plotinus furnishes no hint here of an answer to this question, but begins immediately to speak of the individual soul's seeking to be by itself, its fault in falling from the innocent state in which it governed together with soul-entire, its departure and isolation from the whole, its "looking" to the part, its descent into the tomb of the body (IV, 8, 4, 10–25).

The passage just summarized would seem to indicate that the governance of individual bodies by particular souls can be effected only by the "departure" of these souls from soul-entire. The language used might suggest that this departure is voluntary and avoidable. Plotinus, however, understands it to be necessary. The soul descends by the eternal and necessary law of its own nature (IV, 8, 5, 10–14), for it necessarily has a double life: the life of the intelligible world and the life of the sensible world (IV, 8, 4, 30–35). The descent is free in that it is due to its own nature, but necessitated in that it is due to the necessary law of its own nature; the soul can be said to suffer punishment for what it has done since it itself has done it, even though the descent from the better to the worse is always involuntary. The "crime" which the soul commits by descending into the body is the descent itself, or is the nature of the individual soul itself—the expression is indefinite (IV, 8, 5, 5–18). "Thus indeed the soul, although it is divine and from the regions above, comes to be within the body: the last of gods comes hither by a self-activated fall and by reason of its potency and for the reason of ordering of that which is after it. And if it flees very quickly it is harmed in no way in having taken up in addition knowledge of evil, and in having known the nature of vice, and in having exercised its potencies towards manifestation, and for having caused works and makings to appear . . ." (IV, 8, 5, 24 – 30).

Plotinus is almost saying here that the individual soul can be present to the sensible without contamination, that it comes here only to perform its proper function, the ordering of the body, by using powers which would have been "in vain" *(ibid.,* lines 30 – 33) in the incorporeal world. "The soul is harmed in no way" in doing this, "if it flees very quickly." Yet there is still a sense in which it "should" not have come hither, because "if it flees very quickly" seems to carry with it a residual connotation that the soul is still not at home in the body. But in the context it seems to relate to a previous statement in the same chapter, where it is said that the soul "which enters the body less" and "withdraws sooner" is judged "according to its merits" *(ibid.,* lines 19 – 20). Thus the "moral" fault of the soul—as distinguished from the physical— consists in a plunging more deeply into the body and in a withdrawing later.

Now, to go into the body at all is precisely the "physical" fault of the soul. *These two "faults" are, then, described in the same language, the "moral fault" differing only in degree from the "physical fault."* This reinforces the view that the "physical" fault is, after all, still to be taken as a "fault"—that the word "fault" here has more force than a mere statement of the inferior position of any soul in reference to the Nous.

Plotinus does not wish, any more than Plato did, to say that the ordering of the sensible is due to a "fault." But he is faced with two problems, probably unsolvable on Platonic terms. Soul, to order matter, needs to be involved with matter, because any logos which matter has is due to soul, and is in some way soul. Thus soul seemingly could not function as ordering matter purely "from above," since matter in that case would not have any principles in it capable of being ordered. Thus the necessity for "lower parts" of the individual soul, the "composition" in man of soul and ensouled body, "nature," "logoi produced by nature," etc.

Yet matter is eternally impassible, non-being, evil. The paradoxes develop:

1) Soul does not need matter, yet it has potencies that are realized only in an involvement with matter.

2) Matter stands in need of ordering by the true beings. For the

reasons explained above, this necessitates, in effect, an involvement of soul, the intermediate principle, with matter. But matter is yet impassible, thus incapable of being ordered. Therefore a multiplication of parts of soul, and of logoi, is required in the attempt to do what, it would seem, can never even be begun.

3) Matter stands in eternal need of ordering. This ordering can be accomplished only by the true beings, therefore the orderer of matter, the soul, must be in some way a true being, i.e., must be in some way in the intelligible world. On the other hand, for the reasons explained above, this orderer of matter must become involved in matter, must descend to the evil. And this descent must always be described, in some fashion, as a fault.

Yet Plotinus makes the strongest possible attempts to mitigate these paradoxes, and to establish a proper level for soul, the intermediary between Nous and the sensible world: a level which is *worse,* but not a *worsening.*

That soul is primitively one and many illustrates an important side of Plotinus' thought. The gradation of the One, the One-Many, and the One and Many is eternally fixed, and is an expression of the nature of reality. Soul, and souls, have their own established character, their own place, their own "seat."

Despite strong expressions to the contrary, Plotinus tries not to regard this as a fault, as a culpable falling off from unity. The highest part of the World Soul, eternally blessed, is eternally in the Nous and loses nothing of its blessedness by being soul, by fulfilling its role in governing the sensible universe. It cannot forsake its character as soul and be purely Nous or purely One; it is fixed as soul. Precisely as soul, a particular soul may turn from the body and realize its (already effected) articulation in soul-entire. As we have seen, it may be able to do this without renouncing its governance of the body.

Nature, the lower part of the World Soul, constitutes a level lower than that of soul proper, an eternally fixed level of contemplation which falls short of the clear contemplation of the blessed souls which remain in the Nous. Yet, at least according to the entire "gradation" side of Plotinism, matter could not be formed without this lower part of the World Soul. It seems probable that soul falls short of Nous, then, in this respect also. Not only is it necessarily one and many, but it necessarily has a lower part descending towards matter.

Plotinus is not using a *concept* of soul as a principle of explanation to cover some aspect or aspects of the sensible universe. The sensible world is, in its being, soul. This is indicated by his observation that the name "All" is applied better to the World Soul than to the sensible All (VI, 4, 5, 8–9). Soul, specifically as World Soul, is the being of the sensible universe. This is clear from two facts. First, the being with which Plotinus deals is the being of life, order, and intelligibility. Second, matter is for him non-being (II, 5, 4, 14; II, 5, 5, 13; etc.). It never actually unites with form or with soul (II, 5, 5, 21–22). Thus it is soul which is being in, or rather for or with reference to, the sensible universe. Soul as World Soul is then the order of the sensible universe (cf. IV, 3, 9, 15–17). The "parts" of the soul are "parts" of this order. Since this order is an intelligible order, and intelligible only by reference to Nous, soul is at once in Nous (III, 3, 5, 16–18), dependent upon Nous (V, 1, 7, 41–44), and a falling off from Nous (III, 8, 6, 26). Since this order orders the sensible world, soul is an intermediary bringing the order and intelligible quality of Nous to bear on the sensible world (III, 2, 2, 18–41).

Since the sensible world is a descent from Nous in the direction of matter, Plotinus seems at times to try to diminish and diversify soul to a point where it could unite with matter—but this, according to his own principles, can never be. All diversifications and diminutions of soul are still united far more intimately with the higher parts of soul than with the matter they are said to be "in." Soul functions as an intermediary (IV, 6, 3, 5–21) between a higher world and a lower world, which latter it itself forms and orders according to the intellectual quality of its intermediation, and which has its being in and through this intermediation.

SOUL — POIESIS

Plotinus presents still another view of the relation of soul to what is beneath it. The Soul of the All *produces* the visible cosmos (IV, 3, 6, 2). The universe is never, and never was, without soul. The soul is eternally giving matter its form, its order; the producing of the body of the universe by its soul goes on eternally (IV, 3, 9). In the exposition of this doctrine we can trace a relaxation of the

requirements of poiesis: the immobility of the producer is miti-
gated, and thus its stability in the generation of its product is im-
paired. The soul produces only at the cost of declining in some
measure towards its product. This process of declination is at once
the projection of "parts" from itself.

Plotinus can apply to the soul a formula similar to those used in
describing production by the One and by the Nous: it rests according as it produces; its very act of producing involves its own
stasis, *menei kath' ho poiêsei* (IV, 4, 12, 32). The very act of producing
body is, however, the projecting of a lower part, or parts, of the
soul towards (into) the body, to be the form associated with   matter, to be the form "in" the body (although form never unites with
matter).

Now the producing of lower parts proceeds in such a way that
the immobility of the soul is compromised. So, according to another passage, in contrast to the One and the Nous which remain
immobile in producing,

> The soul does not produce while remaining [immobile], but
> having been moved it generates its image. Looking *there*,
> whence it proceeded, it is filled; proceeding to another and op-
> posite movement it generates its own image: sensation; and in
> plants, nature. Now nothing is parted from or cut off from what
> is before it. Thus the soul seems to advance as far as plants: in a
> certain way it does advance, because there is something of it in
> plants. The whole soul is not in plants, but becoming in plants it
> is in them because it descends to that extent to the inferior, in
> producing another hypostasis by the descent and because of
> good will toward the inferior: for the [part] before this, which
> depends on the Nous, also lets the Nous remain in itself.
>
> (V, 2, 1, 18–28.)

The movement of the soul in producing its image is thus twofold: a movement towards the Nous, and an opposite movement,
presumably towards matter. It is not clear why producing by the
Nous could not have been described in terms of a similar twofold
movement, except that Plotinus wishes to portray the soul, the
properly intermediate hypostasis, as less self-sufficient than the
higher hypostases.

This text speaks of sensation and nature, that is, the lower parts of the soul, as the images of higher soul. In other places ensouled body is said to be the image of soul. Plotinus means that ensouled body is the image of lower soul, the image of an image, so that ensouled body is indirectly the image of higher soul.

For the ensouled body, to be the image of soul, to be formed by soul, to be ordered by soul (cf. IV, 3, 27), and to be "made" by soul are all the same. The soul, in producing lower souls for body, forms and orders body and produces body as its image.

The soul seems to advance to plants, because the lower, or vegetative, soul which is in plants is continuous with the higher soul. But the advance of soul to plants is, automatically, the producing of another hypostasis; that is, the soul produces plants in producing, or projecting, an inferior part of itself—the plant soul.

Does the higher part of the soul remain immobile in producing? Apparently not, since it would appear that the higher part is meant in the expressions "The soul does not produce while remaining immobile . . . proceeding to another and opposite movement it generates its own image: sensation; and in plants, nature"— sensation and nature are the images of the higher soul. Yet the movement is described as a *seeming* advance: the higher part does not come to be in plants, but rather produces a lower part for plants. Plotinus is describing an inferior kind of poiesis, a declination from the type of producing effected by the One and by the Nous. The higher hypostases remain immobile in producing, but im-mobility must be at once preserved and relaxed in the case of soul.

For the doctrine of the producing of the body by the soul, one fact, however, emerges from all these considerations: the producing of the body involves some procession of some souls, or parts of soul. As Plotinus describes this process in another place,

Soul-entire is always above, in that in which it is its nature to be. That which is in order from it is the All, illuminated as it were by nearness, as that which is under the sun is illuminated. Now the partial soul is illuminated in being borne towards that which is before it—for then it converses with being. When borne towards that which is after itself, it is borne towards non-being. This is what happens when it is towards itself, for when it wishes towards itself it produces that which is after it, its image, non-being; it itself stumbling and becoming most indefinite: and the image of this image is the indefinite and the entirely dark, for it is altogether devoid of intellect and logos, and stands far aloof from being. Towards this it is still inter-mediate, that is, in its proper place, but looking again, as it were by a second glance, it forms the image, and, being pleased, it goes towards it.   (III, 9, 3, 5–16.)

The general picture is the same here as in texts mentioned above. A higher soul remains with the Nous; the production of body involves the descent of a lower ("partial") soul to form or order matter. The lower soul is in an intermediate position: directed to the higher soul, to itself, to non-being. "When it wishes towards itself it produces . . . its image, non-being." Is the non-being of matter meant here, or the relative non-being of the ensouled body? Taking the expression "the image of this image" to mean that the lower soul is the image of the higher soul, and that the image spoken of here is therefore the produced image of the lower soul, we find the product of the lower soul described as "altogether devoid of intellect and logos," which could be a description of matter alone.

This interpretation is reinforced by what immediately follows. The lower soul "looks again" at the already produced product to *form* it. Plotinus seems to be saying that the lower soul, by a first glance, produces matter; by a second glance forms it, that is, makes it to be body. The producing of matter is done only at the cost of the lower soul's "stumbling and becoming most indefinite." This phrase expresses very forcefully his usual thought that soul is denigrated by close association with matter or with body. Here the denigration is noteworthy because it is taken to be the condition of the producing of body. Lower soul, according to this text at least, produces only at the cost of a declination in itself, "stumbling and becoming most indefinite."[10]

The notion of a two-step producing of body figures also in Plotinus' description of the producing of the universe by the World Soul: "If body were not, the soul would not proceed, since there is no other place in which it is natural for the soul to be. If it is to proceed, it will generate a place for itself, and thus a body. Now the soul . . . is like a huge light, which, shining to its uttermost limits, becomes darkness. The soul, seeing this darkness, which it has made subsist, forms this darkness."[11] But in this passage there is no mention of stumbling, or becoming indefinite. As the World Soul can govern the universe without contamination, so it can produce it without stumbling.

The Nous is productive, and its producing is intelligent, but it does not produce by deliberating or by discursive reasoning. Similarly, the World Soul produces "according to ideas" (II, 3, 17, 13) but without any "deliberation brought in from outside itself," without "waiting to examine" (IV, 3, 10, 15), and, like the Nous, without logismos (IV, 4, 10, 27–29). In governing its world, it does not employ dianoia, discursive reasoning, nor does it have to correct anything (II, 9, 2, 12–18): it produces in a uniform and consistent way, not by accident, but because it knows what is to be, and orders its inferiors according to the pattern it has in itself (IV, 4, 12, 29–36).

Plotinus is faithful here to his own notion of poiesis. Poiesis is always to some degree intelligent, or better noetic, theoretic: this is true even in the case of nature's poiesis. It is not deliberative. Deliberative making is not natural, but according to an adventitious art, which produces obscure and weak imitations (IV, 3, 10, 16–17). Thus, just as the poiesis effected by Nous was superior to that   effected by art, so too is the World Soul's working superior to the working of art.

SOUL—THEORIA

Since nature is the lower part of the World Soul, contemplation by the higher part of this soul furnishes the instance of contemplation immediately prior to nature's.

The World Soul produces and governs the visible universe by a vision, a contemplation: "The Soul of the All has given to every body to have as much as this body can have from it. It remains without practical activity (*apragmonôs*), not governing by discursive reason or correcting anything, but ordering by a contemplation towards that which is before it, by marvelous power. As much as it is directed to this contemplation, so much is it more beautiful and more powerful: having from thence, it gives to what is after it, and as it illuminates, so is it eternally illumined." (II, 9, 2, 12–18.)

The notion that the World Soul gives body as much as body can receive is the notion, found in Plotinus before Proclus, that what is received is received according to the ability of the receiver. The World Soul does not work by "practical" activity in Plotinus' sense, that is, it works not because of want but because of superabundance. It orders all things by a vision of the Nous; working by this vision it produces and governs. It acts either directly upon body, or upon its own lower part, nature, and through nature, upon body.

The "vision" by which the World Soul produces and governs is not an affair of discursive reason. This point was established above, where it was shown in passing that the knowledge by which the World Soul produces is not logismos or dianoia. It deserves more detailed treatment here, because it will enable us to show that several passages dealing with contemplation by soul refer primarily, not to the World Soul, but to the human soul.

Ennead IV, 4, 10–12, a group of chapters principally directed towards showing that the Soul of the All has no need of memory, demonstrates also the subsidiary point that it does not employ discursive reasoning. It does not go through a process of seeking and discovery, but possesses its wisdom in an eternal changelessness (IV, 4, 10, 7–15; IV, 4, 12, 5–18). The fact that it produces many and varied things is no reason why it should change: the more varied the products, the more does the producer remain fixed (IV, 4, 11, 14–17). The knowledge which the World Soul has is one, self-identical, an eternal wisdom (*ibid.*, lines 23–27). We see that the World Soul is not a discoverer or cognitive receiver of the things that come after it, but rather their theoretic-poietic producer.

But while the wisdom of the World Soul is above discursive reasoning, its contemplating still falls short of the wisdom of the Nous. In its contemplating, as in its nature, it occupies an intermediate position: "With regard to what is called the Soul of the All, it was never engaged in evil work, it does not suffer evils, but is a contemplation which both considers (*perinoein*) those things which are below it and hangs ever from those things which are above it, as much as the two are possible simultaneously; it takes from thence [the intelligible world], and directs *this* world simultaneously, since, being soul, it is impossible that it not reach to them [to the things of this world]." (IV, 8, 7, 26–32.)

Immediately before this passage, Plotinus had been speaking of human souls, which come to a knowledge of good from an experience of evil. He says here that this is not true of the Soul of the All. To call the World Soul "a contemplation which both considers those things which are below it and hangs ever from those things which are above it" is to display the World Soul once more as intermediate between the visible universe and the Nous: this is true even if the first function be appropriated to the lower part and the second to the higher, since both functions are in between the world and the Nous.

The World Soul "considers those things which are below it." In view of the fact that the World Soul both produces and governs the world, the "consideration" mentioned here cannot be caused, or conditioned, by "the things which are below it." Thus this "consideration" can be neither sensation, which in Plotinus' view involves a "receiving" from the sensible world (cf. IV, 3, 26, 5–9; V, 5, 1, 61–65) and is therefore posterior to it, nor the discursive reasoning which is based upon sensation. The "consideration" here must rather be the World Soul's eternal wisdom.

A contemplation which considers the world and depends always upon the Nous: the expression here is different from that of II, 9, 2, where the World Soul is said to order the world by contemplating the Nous. Here the contemplation might seem at first glance to be directed primarily towards the world. This, however, need not be Plotinus' meaning. In contemplating the Nous, the World Soul knows the world as the imitation of the Nous, an imitation which it is its function to produce.

The phrase "as much as the two are possible simultaneously" seems intended to convey some note of a schism in the functioning of the World Soul. Yet the World Soul encounters no obstacle in governing the world; it orders the visible universe with marvelous power (II, 9, 2, 14–15), it governs the world easily (IV, 8, 2, 24). The word "simultaneously" is not meant temporally, but indicates the internal duality of the World Soul. The suggestion of a schism can point only to the inferiority of soul with reference to the Nous, its relatively looser unity. As soul, performing its proper function of mediation, it must "reach to the things of this world"; and it must simultaneously maintain its dependence on the Nous. Only by its dependence on the Nous does it order the visible cosmos; yet its dependence on the Nous is not precisely the same as its ordering of the world: it has two faces, two parts; their mutual union is not so close as the internal unity of the Nous. Thus it would appear that the knowing and contemplating activities of the World Soul are not reasoning, yet they are like reasoning in that they form a link between the intelligible and the sensible.

We might expect a treatment of World Soul's contemplation, one that differentiates this contemplation both from Nous and from discursive reasoning, in Plotinus' treatise on contemplation, *Ennead* III, 8. But in III, 8, 5, where he begins to talk of contemplation on the part of soul, many expressions seem to indicate that Plotinus is talking of discursive reasoning, and, consequently, of the contemplation appropriate to a soul other than the Soul of the All: "But now that we have said, with regard to nature, how its generating is a contemplation, let us come to the soul, which is before it, and say how its contemplation, its love for learning, its seeking, its urge for producing from what it knows and its fullness, cause it, since it has become altogether a *theorema*, to produce another *theorema*. . . ." (III, 8, 5, 1–6.)

The expression "the soul which is before nature" would be especially applicable to the higher part of the World Soul; it is applicable also to the human soul, in the sense that the human soul, at least its highest part, is a type of soul superior to nature. But in view of the passages from IV, 4, to which allusion has been made above, the phrases "love of learning" and "seeking" do not characterize the World Soul: it has been Plotinus' explicit doctrine that the World Soul does not *seek* to know, but knows. The soul which learns is not the eternally fixed World Soul, but the human soul.

The immediately subsequent phrases "its urge for producing from what it knows" and "its fullness" could be appropriated to the World Soul.

"Since it has become altogether a theorema" is a literal rendering of the original: *autên theôrêma pan gegomenên*; this is not
explained either in the context or in the immediately following
text, but in virtue of Plotinus' general doctrine that when a veritable reality contemplates it produces another thing as its
theorema (III, 8, 7, 1–3), the phrase in question probably means
that the soul has been produced, in its complete reality, as the
theorema of the Nous. The soul makes "another theorema"—
apparently an inferior part of itself. After citing the analogy of the
master's knowledge causing knowledge in the pupil, Plotinus
proceeds: "The rational part (*to logistikon*) of the soul is above, and
towards the above; ever filled and enlightened it remains there:
the other part of the soul participates in this, which has partici-
pated in the first participation." [12]

A soul is being spoken of, a soul with two parts, the higher
of which is called the "*rational.*" In V, 3, the second treatise before
this one in the chronological order, Plotinus has dealt with the
"rational." It is the highest faculty properly *in us,* the faculty by
which *we* judge images issuing from sensation according to the
rule furnished by the Nous (V, 3, 3, 6–9). The Nous is not counted
among the parts of our soul: it is ours only when we use it (*ibid.,*
lines 23–28). "We are not the Nous: we are according to the Nous
by the rational part of the soul (*to logistikon*), that first receives
[from the Nous] . . . . This is what we are: . . . the principal part
of the soul (*to kurion tês psychês*), intermediate between two powers
. . . the worse the power of sensation, the better, the Nous." (*Ibid.,*
lines 31–39.)

Plotinus, then, understands by the rational part of the soul
something proper to human knowing, something which is not at
all the same as the abiding wisdom of the World Soul. Since, then,
the highest part of the soul spoken of in III, 8, 5, is this rational part,
there is strong reason for supposing that the soul referred to here is
the human soul.

And yet, despite the weight to be attached to such phrases as
"love of learning," "seeking," and "the reasoning power," it is still
not perfectly certain that Plotinus is speaking of the human soul in
III, 8, 5. Certain expressions in the lines immediately following

those just discussed suggest rather the World Soul: "the soul (or lower part thereof) reaches everywhere and there is no place where it is absent"; "since then the soul becomes everywhere and there is nowhere where its act is not . . ." (III, 8, 5, 13–17). It is possible, however, that Plotinus is speaking here of the presence of the individual soul everywhere in the individual body.

Ennead III, 8, 5, in which, ultimately, we cannot be certain of which soul Plotinus is speaking, is followed at once by a chapter dealing with praxis and learning, to show how they are contemplations and lead to contemplation: a section clearly referring only to the human soul.

The detailed exposition of Plotinus' chapter on the soul's contemplating has led us, therefore, to this conclusion: the treatise on contemplation does not contain a specific presentation of contemplation by the World Soul which is at once elaborate and applicable beyond doubt to the World Soul. Therefore, for the doctrine of the World Soul's contemplation, we are dependent on:

1) The short unequivocal passage from II, 9, 2, quoted on pages 62–63 *supra.*

2) The doctrine of the World Soul's kind of knowledge, its "wisdom," contained in IV, 4, 10–12, treated on page 63–64 *supra.*

3) Parallels that can be drawn between nature's contemplation and soul's contemplation, and hints about soul's contemplation derivable from the treatments of the contemplations appropriate to Nous and nature.

4) The indications of the contemplation appropriate to the World Soul which can be gained from III, 8, 7. This chapter, summarizing previous sections, contains several general observations on contemplation. Since, however, the previous chapters have not treated contemplation in nature and in the higher part of the World Soul, but rather, it would seem, contemplation in nature and in the human soul, even those general observations should be applied to the higher part of the World Soul only with caution:

That all things, including those that are truly beings, are from contemplation and are themselves contemplation is now clear. Theoremata likewise are those things which are generated from

true beings when they themselves contemplate: some are
theoremata for sensation, some for knowledge, some for opinion. Actions aim toward knowledge as their end, and desire is
desire of knowledge. Generatings proceed from contemplation
and terminate in a form, which is another theorema. And in
general, since everything is an imitation of the producing
beings, it produces theoremata, which is to say, forms; and generated entities, being the imitations of beings, show that the
purpose of producing beings is not producings or practical
actions but the result itself—that it may be contemplated. This is
what acts of discursive thought (*dianoêseis*) wish to see, as before
them do sensations, whose end is knowledge; and before sensations, nature produces within herself a theorema, which is a
logos, and brings to completion another logos.   (III, 8, 7, 1–14.)

"All things, including those that are truly beings, are from contemplation and are themselves contemplation." Applied to soul,
this sentence would seem to mean:

1) That the soul is *from* the self-contemplation of the Nous. On
this point we may observe that there is no specific development of
this theme in the present treatise.

2) That the soul is itself a contemplation. Here again a difficulty
arises from the doctrine of III, 8, 8, that in the ascent of contemplation from nature to soul to Nous the contemplations become ever
more closely united to the contemplators (III, 8, 8, 1–4). Soul
would appear to be a contemplator which is not united to its act of
contemplating—how then can it be said simply *to be* a contemplation? Yet nature likewise is called, simply, a contemplation.

"Theoremata likewise are those things which are generated
from true beings when they themselves contemplate . . ." This expression, taken by itself, would justify our saying that the soul is
the theorema of the Nous. The next phrase, however, throws some
doubt on the plausibility of this interpretation. "Some are
theoremata for sensation, some for knowledge, some for opinion."
In the first place, the enumeration appears to be an enumeration of
activities of the *human* soul, in which case the whole sentence
would mean only that the true beings, in contemplating, generate

theoremata for the human soul. But what are theoremata? We recall that, from its composition, the word "theorema" can mean either *object* of contemplation or *work* of contemplation. In III, 8, 8, in the allusions to the *internal* theorema of the Nous, it apparently means object of contemplation. What is its meaning here?

A work of contemplation could be conceivably also an object of contemplation, either for the being which produces it, or for another. From III, 8, 6, it would appear that ordinary human productive activity, praxis, has as its end the production of a work, a theorema, which can then be contemplated by the worker.

Now when the Nous, at least, contemplates-generates, that which it generates is not its own object of contemplation. The Nous is self-knowledge, it is its own object. It is true that it knows its imitations in knowing itself, but this would not, without a great deal of qualification, justify calling these imitations the objects of the Nous' knowledge.

The higher part of the World Soul has a relative completeness which would seem to preclude the possibility of its generating either nature or the visible cosmos as an object of contemplation. Its object of contemplation would appear to be in one way the Nous, in another way itself. It must, then, generate nature and, through nature, body, as works of contemplation.

On the other hand, the World Soul, in its function of ordering the visible cosmos, is the being of the visible cosmos. In this sense, its object of contemplation could be said to be body; but only because the being of body is soul. Thus even in this function, its function as nature, soul is its own object of contemplation.

It would seem that the only cases where the object of contemplation could be other than the contemplator are those where a work of contemplation, projected outside *this* contemplator either by the contemplator or by a higher hypostasis, is to be assimilated to this contemplator for the contemplator's enhancement. This condition obtains only in praxis and in learning. In praxis the operator makes for himself an object of contemplation; in the case of learning, objects of contemplation, coming to the human soul from without, are assimilated to the soul itself. But nature does not require these prolegomena to contemplation, so, *a fortiori,* neither does the World Soul. The Nous, the higher part of the World Soul, and nature do not produce objects of contemplation for themselves, but rather, as contemplative producers, works of contemplation.

Therefore, it appears that the passage in question says two things:

1) That producing beings produce *works* of contemplation.

2) That these, or some of these, *works* of contemplation are *objects* of contemplation for the human soul.

"Theorema" is intended in these two senses in the second sentence: the *works* of contemplation, generated by the true beings, are *objects* of contemplation for human sensation, knowledge, and opinion.[13]

The subsequent sentences show an intermingling of the two themes. Generatings terminate in a work of contemplation; everything, as an imitation of the contemplative producing beings, produces a work of contemplation. But that "actions aim toward knowledge as their end" is to be understood, in the light of III, 8, 6, to mean that ordinary human productive actions produce works of contemplation, which in turn are, for their producers, objects of contemplation.

". . . Generated entities, being the imitations of beings, show that the purpose of the producing beings is not producings or practical actions but the result itself—that it may be contemplated." It would be difficult to take this expression to mean that the generated entities in the visible cosmos, the imitations of the true beings in the Nous, show that the purpose of the true beings is that these generated entities be contemplated, since, as has been said, the generating of the visible cosmos does not produce precisely an object of contemplation either for the Nous or for the Soul of the All, and it does not seem likely that Plotinus can mean that the simple *purpose* of Nous or the World Soul in projecting them is to furnish objects of contemplation for the human soul. It might seem that Plotinus refers once more to human practical activity and its projection of a work-object of contemplation.

The next sentence lends some support to this interpretation, but raises further questions. Acts of discursive thought wish to see results that may be contemplated—this may mean that discursive thought, relatively disunited, has for its end contemplation, and, by a quasi-practical action, projects parts that will later be united in contemplation. Sensation has this nisus towards contemplation, and it too is a projection for the sake of subsequent unification. The mention of discursive thought and of sensation here recalls the observations on learning in III, 8, 6, and reinforces the view that Plotinus' main concern in the entire treatment of contemplation as it pertains to the soul is to show how the activities of the *human* soul are directed towards contemplation.

In the last sentence, nature is listed with the powers of the human soul, and is placed "before," that is, in this case, *below* sensation. The implication is important. On the one hand, Plotinus has given no clear doctrine of contemplation in the higher part of the World Soul, or in soul entire, a contemplation which could serve as a link between that appropriate to the Nous and that appropriate to nature. In its place, the section on contemplation in "the soul before (above) nature" has been devoted to the relation to contemplation of various parts and powers of the human soul: now, as the section draws to a close, nature is assigned a position among the powers of the human soul.

The issue of this for Plotinus' doctrine of nature will be discussed in chapter 6. Here only a provisional determination can be made: nature's contemplation must be in some way inferior to that connected with discursive reasoning, learning, sensation, and practical activity.

In sum, the contemplating appropriate to the Soul of the All is a changeless eternal wisdom which produces the sensible world as its work of contemplation, while remaining in its higher part immobile. The cognitive activity by which the human soul is characteristically itself is logismos, which can produce external works of contemplation by praxis, and perhaps internal works of contemplation by itself. Both of these contemplators-producers seem, up to this point, to be superior to nature as a contemplative producer.

NOTES

1. III, 3, 5, 16–18; cf. II, 5, 3, 31–33; III, 4, 3, 21–28.

2. V, 9, 4, 15–19. For the meaning and importance of "self-identical" in Plotinus' philosophy, *vide infra*, pp. 104 ff.

3. Cf. III, 9, 3, 1–4; IV, 3, 9, 34–51; VI, 4, 5, 8–11. "Body is in soul" is Plotinus' deliberate technical expression, and should counteract occasional lapses such as that implied in V, 9, 4, 15–19.

4. Soul-entire is designated, e.g., *hê pasa psychê*, III, 9, 3, 1; *hê mia hê holê*, VI, 4, 4, 41. World Soul is *hê tou pantos*, IV, 8, 7, 27; *hê tou holou*, IV, 3, 8, 3, etc.

5. VI, 5, 9, 11–12; IV, 4, 14, 1–9; cf. VI, 4, 4, 34–36.

6. Thus the "perfect soul" alluded to in IV, 8, 2, 20 (quoted and commented on *infra*, p. 53) can be, according to the context, both all soul and Soul of the All, or either one (cf. III, 4, 2, 1). But if soul-entire is identified with the soul of the visible cosmos, there is a danger that man will be seen as merely a part of the cosmos, his life controlled by the influence of the stars, etc. So, according to some passages, our higher, "divine" soul does not come from (is not a part of) the Soul of the All (cf. IV, 3, 27).

7. There is no doubt that some souls are contaminated by their connection with matter; the point is whether any *need* be. Armstrong's statement, "There is, I think, no passage in the *Enneads* where Soul or souls are said to be spoilt or thwarted by *hylê*," fails to take into account several texts. (Arthur Hilary Armstrong, *The Architecture of the Intelligible Universe in the Philosophy of Plotinus*, Cambridge, England, 1940, p. 90.) Plotinus says, "The nature of bodies, to the extent that it participates in matter, is evil . . . it is an obstacle to the proper activity of soul . . ." (I, 8, 4, 1–4); and, specifically of the evil soul, "Further, if its rational part is troubled, it is prevented from seeing by the passions and by matter overshadowing it, and it declines towards matter, and it looks wholly not towards being (*ousian*), but towards becoming, of which the principle is the nature of matter, which is so evil that it contaminates (*anapimplanai*) with its evil that which is not yet in it, but only looks towards it. Not having any part of good, void of all, the extreme

deficiency, matter renders like itself everything that has the least contact with it." (*Ibid.,* lines 17–25.)

8. *hôs:* Ficino, probably having in mind the recurrence of uncertainties on this point, translates as "quasi."

9. IV, 8, 2, 19–26. "Traverses the heavens and governs the cosmos" is an allusion to *Phaedrus,* 246c, but the specific application to "our " soul and the subsequent explanations are entirely Plotinus'.

10. The identity of the lower soul, the activity of which is described in this passage, is not obvious. Plotinus contrasts it to soul-entire (*hê pasa psychê*), and calls it *hê merikê,* the "partial." Bréhier ("Notice" to III, 9, in his edition of the *Enneads,* III, 170) takes this to mean a part of the soul, presumably a part of the Soul of the All. But it could mean *the individual soul.*

There are difficulties with either rendering. The notion of an individual soul producing its own body would seem incompatible with IV, 3, 6, 1–8 (the doctrine that the Soul of the All produces the world, while individual souls only administer it). On the other hand, the expression "being pleased [with its image] it goes toward it" is clearly reminiscent of Plotinus' usual doctrine of the fall of the individual soul because of an attraction for the body.

11. IV, 3, 9, 20–26. Cf. III, 4, 1.

12. III, 8, 5, 10–12. *To logistikon* was deleted by Kirchhoff, who supplied a new subject for the sentence, *to prôton,* from the end of the immediately preceding sentence by altering the position of the period. He was followed in this by subsequent editors until Henry. The deletion of *to logistikon* is without manuscript authority. Even if the reading *to prôton* were accepted, it is in itself ambiguous, while the expressions "love of learning" and "seeking" would still suggest strongly that the passage deals with the *human* soul. (*Vide* Henry, app. crit. ad III, 8, 5; cp. A. Kirchhoff, ed., *Plotini Opera,* Leipzig, 1856, 30 [Kirchhoff follows the chronological order of the treatises], 5.)

13. Ficino's translation brings this point out: ". . . his videlicet contemplantibus ipsa facta jam contemplamina, vel sensui, vel cognitioni, vel opinioni passim se offerentia."

5

PLOTINUS' account of the production and governance of the visible universe through the poiesis-theoria of the Nous, the soul, and nature gains a new dimension from the incorporation into his thought of a freshly conceived notion of logos.

The doctrine of logos, as it appears throughout the *Enneads*, especially in III, 2, clearly owes much to the Stoics. Plotinus, however, acclimatizes logos to his philosophy by treating it as an immaterial principle, and by articulating the notion with the scheme of the hypostases. It is not itself an hypostasis,[1] but an aspect of Nous, of soul, of nature. In Plotinus' remolding of the Stoic doctrine, the reasonableness of the world becomes the presence of intellectuality in all things. Nous and soul are each a logos and a sum of logoi. Nature is a logos. Logos is not a distinct hypostasis, but the intellectuality present in everything from the Nous downwards.

LOGOS—NOUS

According to Plotinus' doctrine in *Ennead* VI, 4, the Nous is, as it were, one logos. But the Nous is being, and otherness is appropriated to being and not to non-being: the one of being is never absent from it. Thus the Nous is many and various, but *as* various and many, it is one. The Nous, one logos, which is real being, contains many logoi, which are real beings.[2]

The intelligible world, the Nous, is solely logos (III, 2, 2, 36), and "Nous, then, immobile and at rest, giving something of itself towards matter, fashioned all things. This logos flows forth from

Nous. For that which flows forth from Nous is logos, and it flows forth always, so long as Nous is present in things." (*Ibid.*, lines 15 – 18.)

According to this text, the influence of Nous upon its inferiors generally, and upon matter particularly, is a flowing-forth of logos. Plotinus does not say that Nous as logos flows forth, or that the logoi within Nous flow forth. Nous remains immobile and at rest. Logos (in some sense yet to be determined) flows forth, and its doing so brings it about that Nous is present in all things. In other words, logos is the vehicle of something of Nous, bringing about a presence of Nous in its inferiors.

When Plotinus describes the soul as logos and logoi, the language he uses shows the diminution of intellectuality, and the relaxation of unity in the direction of the sensible All, in the descent from Nous to soul. The soul is the logos of the Nous but, as the image of the Nous, it is an obscure logos. It is a logos, and in a way a Nous, but it looks to another—that is to say, it contemplates *the* Nous, in comparison to which it is deficient (V, 1, 6, 44 – 48). Logos, coming from the Nous, makes the soul to be knowing (II, 9, 1, 31–33)—a clear indication that logos is intellectuality.[3]

The Nous supplies and fills the soul with logoi (III, 5, 9, 30), fitting it for the production of the sensible All. In the soul, as in the Nous, all the logoi are together, but they are, as it were, further relaxed and ready for deployment. They are separated in the soul's product, the visible cosmos (cf. III, 2, 17, 74–79; IV, 4, 16, 4–9).

The soul is at rest in itself, easily governing the sensible All according to reason. Yet logos, reason, the expression of the primitive through-and-through duality of the Nous, is "different in relation to itself" (i.e., composed of the same and the other), and so produces the maximum otherness, contrariety (III, 2, 16, 45–58). This contrariety is resolved and at peace in the Nous and in the soul, but in the sensible All it finds expression as a war of logoi, as a development with collisions and mutual impedances (cf. *ibid.*, lines 28 – 41).

This is to say that the sensible All presents itself as a world in which things are opposed to one another, in which there is a strife of the good and the worse. This ultimate expression of logos as contrariety does not, however, destroy logos as order. The opposing logoi finding deployment in the sensible All are ordered by the Soul of the All in its aspect of *one logos*. The logos of the All is like the governance of a city, and like a harmonizing drama in which the individual souls and logoi are the actors (cf. III, 2, 17).

The rule of logos in the visible universe, a rule guaranteed by the fact that the soul, the emissary of the Nous, and the vehicle of logos from the Nous, is the being of the visible universe, is, in Plotinus' treatment, equated with providence. For Plotinus, providence is simply the intellectuality of the universe, the presence of logos in it, and its governance by logos as the representative of Nous. It is not an anthropomorphic care for the world by the higher hypostases, nor is it precisely foreknowledge, or even knowledge, of the visible universe by the Nous. The visible universe is not an object of knowledge for the Nous: the Nous knows itself, and produces the visible universe through the intermediation of soul, the vehicle of logos and logoi, as an intellectual production. It is "foreknown" only in the sense that knowledge, which is the Nous, is metaphysically prior to it as its cause.

Plotinus' reasoning here rests on a firm conviction of the goodness and intellectuality of real being. Evil men, noxious beasts, etc., not only do not escape the order of world logos, but must have a part to play in that order. He makes only a slight attempt to show *a posteriori* what that part is.

The soul's producing of the sensible universe, treated in our previous chapter, can now be assessed further from the aspect logos. The soul, as a logos and sum of logoi, is unquiet (cf. III, 7, 11, 20–23). In a striking passage, Plotinus says that its entity is the potency of logoi, and when it acts, according to its entity, towards other things, that is, towards the sensible All, its act is "logoi" (VI, 2, 5, 12–15). Since it acts towards the sensible All by producing it, this passage means that its producing of the sensible All, its forming of the visible cosmos, is a "logizing"—an ordering according to reason. To say that the entity of the soul is a potency of logoi means, in this connection, that the soul is pregnant with the "dispersed" logoi of the sensible All.

This is borne out again in the several passages where Plotinus

compares the activity of the soul to the functioning of the spermatic logos in the individual animal (IV, 3, 10, 7–13). Just as the
spermatic logos brings about an unfolding into unequal but co-
ordinated parts, so the Soul of the All, as a logos, brings about a
non-homogeneous but ordered universe.

Considered as the universal logos, the Soul of the All is a paradigm (cf. V, 7, 1, 15), a prefiguration of the world order, an intellectual illumination in the direction of matter (cf. IV, 3, 10, 7–13).
What the World Soul prefigures, the individual souls accomplish
according to the prefiguration, or, as in a drama, they act out their
parts as the World Soul prepares these parts.[4]

The assignment of parts in the world drama is, of course, a par-
titioning of logoi. Although, according to one passage, all the logoi
which are present in the World Soul are present in each individual
soul, all are not simultaneously active there (V, 7, 1, 7–10).

The visible universe is the encounter of logos with matter. Matter, non-being, is the root of both blind chance and blind necessity.
Both are *alogia*, "unreasonableness."[5] Logos, the forming and
ordering intellectual principle, dominates matter in the direction
of order and goodness. The visible universe is good and beautiful
insofar as it has any trace of being, because for Plotinus a trace of
being is a trace of Nous, a trace of intellectuality: in a word, *logos*.

Plotinus' theme in this treatment of the visible universe is the
same one which will appear later, in a different guise, as the
participation of matter in the intelligibles. Working out certain
strong suggestions he finds in Plato, but surpassing his Platonic
inspiration, he argues, with innumerable shifts of phrase and illustration, that what is in any way "being" in the visible world is
the trace of intelligence found there. His meaning is that soul
and nature, each in its turn a logos and a bearer of logoi, cause
intellectuality, a diminished intellectuality, to shine on the obscurity of matter. And to say that the visible universe is produced
by logos and is, in its reality, a deployment of logoi, is, for Plotinus,
to say that it is produced by contemplation, by nature contemplating. The identification of producing-governing by logos with
producing by contemplation cannot be strange when we consider
that logos is intellectuality, and beneath the Nous, diminished

intellectuality. To produce, to produce a form, that is, to form, is to fill things with logoi, to make them works of contemplation: in a word, to contemplate (cf. III, 8, 7, 18–21).

But is there not a disparity between logos as diversifying intellectuality and contemplation as resting and stable? Not entirely, for Nous, even considered as a logos containing logoi, is at rest. So also, comparatively speaking, is soul (cf. III, 8, 6, 10–11). And for its part, contemplation also involves duality, the duality of contemplation and contemplator.

The soul, containing the logoi of all things in the visible universe, gives logoi to the bodies of the visible universe (cf. IV, 3, 10, 38–42). This giving of logoi is the producing of these bodies; that is, a body, together with its size and extension, is brought about by a coming of logos upon matter (cf. IV, 7, 2, 22–25). This coming of logos is, from different aspects, a coming of unit, of form, of beauty, of life (cf. 1, 6, 2, 13–24; IV, 3, 10, 38 - 42). The trace of unity is the trace of the unified Nous, and ultimately of the One; the trace of form and beauty is the trace of intellectual being, and so again of the Nous; the trace of soul is the imitation of life.

An individual soul is, like the Soul of the All, a logos and a sum of logoi. In this connection Plotinus frequently, though not always, used the Stoic expressions "spermatic logos" and "logoi in the seed."[6] But these logoi are diminished actualities as are any logoi beneath Nous. The development of a living thing from a seed thus becomes an instance of proliferation of co-ordinated and "unequal" logoi in the material universe, and as such can serve as an illustration of the eternal production of the entire sensible All by the World Soul as logos.

Logos, given by soul, proceeding from soul, "comes upon" matter (IV, 7, 2, 22–25). Expressions such as this might make one think of logos as an intermediary between soul and matter. That is not the case, and for two reasons. First, logos, although it is often convenient both for Plotinus and for a commentator on him to speak of it substantively, is always an aspect of soul, always the World Soul or an individual soul as the bearer of a proliferating, diminished intellectuality. Thus to say that logos "from" soul comes upon matter means that soul, as an intellectual orderer, comes upon matter. Second, matter, the matter which logos is said to order, adorn, and unify, remains for Plotinus *impassible* non-being. Logos does not, any more than soul, really unite with matter. To consider the soul as logos serves to display it more cogently as the fashioner of, and the reality of, the visible cosmos, but not to bring it any closer to a union with matter.

Plotinus does make attempts to surmount the barrier between soul-logos and matter. He speaks in one place of a fitting of matter to logos by logos: "And let us say that the logos has in itself also the logos of the matter. It works over the matter for itself, making it according to itself, or *finding* it harmonious. For the logos of an ox is not upon any other matter but the matter of an ox . . ." (III, 3, 4, 37–41).

This passage occurs in a place where Plotinus is explaining that the deficiencies of deficient men are not to be attributed to their particular matters, since the particular soul has a matter befitting itself. In the quoted excerpt there is the arresting suggestion that logos or soul actually changes matter, actually fits it to itself, *informs* it in an Aristotelian sense. This is, however, weakened by the alternative "or finding it harmonious."

The initial phrase "the logos of the matter" implies that matter itself has a *raison*, an intellectuality, and is not, after all, inert non-being, and this in turn recalls that Plotinus said once that it is "the last of forms" (V, 8, 7, 22–23).

Plotinus' reworking of the notion of logos enables it to serve as the focus of intellectuality *vis-a-vis* proliferation in the descent from the Nous. Logos is reason as co-ordinated intellectual interplay, it is intellectuality in its successive involvements with multiplicity as it descends to the ultimate multiplicity of the visible cosmos. Logos is an articulation of logoi, an ordered intellectuality which appears in successive stages: in its highest form in the Nous, diminished and with a further proliferation in the soul, imitated and still further dispersed in nature and in the sensible All.

Intellectuality must descend from the Nous. "The Nous was not so constituted as to be the last of things" (III, 2, 2, 9–10). It can descend only by diversifying; without further diversification it would remain the relative unity of the Nous. But it can remain intellectual by *ordering* the diversification.

Further, there is an urge for diversification, as well as for unity, in intellectuality itself. Intellectuality is necessarily duality, the duality of knower and known. As it first appears in the Nous, it has not achieved the full diversification of which it is capable. Thus intellectuality itself demands further diversification, in things lower than the Nous, even though this diversification is attained at the expense of a diminution of intellectual quality.

Such are the various and mutually balancing strains Plotinus incorporates in "logos." Logos is the diversifying aspect of intellectuality; it is intellectuality in the devolving process of diversification. Understood this way, it is no stranger to his philosophy, nor is it alien to the scheme of the hypostases. The progression of things from the Nous is an irradiation of intellectuality. The soul, its higher part in the Nous, its lower part bringing about a reflection of intellectuality on matter, is a vehicle for the diversifying intellectuality, the logos, that descends from Nous. [7]

NOTES

1. "Logos . . . does not constitute . . . another nature between Nous and soul" (II, 9, 1, 31–33). This quotation, taken from the treatise called "Against the Gnostics," wherein Plotinus argues generally against the undue multiplication of hypostases, seems to represent his usual position, as the present chapter will attempt to demonstrate. It is true that in III, 5, 9, 20, in the interpretation of a myth, logos is called incidentally "an hypostasis after (*meta*, "post") the Nous." Armstrong, who holds that logos is an hypostasis (p. 102), does not allude to either of these texts, but seems to base himself only on the theory that, in the treatises "On Providence," logos takes over the functions of the World Soul with regard to the visible cosmos. On this latter point, *vide infra*, n. 7.

2. The foregoing paragraph paraphrases the doctrine of VI, 4, 11, 15–20. Cf. II, 4, 16, 2, where logoi are called *ta onta kuriôs*.

3. Cf. III, 8, 8, 16: "How are [the various kinds of life] knowledges? Because they are logoi."

4. VI, 7, 7, 8–16; cf. III, 2, 16, 32–41; III, 2, 17, 32–39.

5. Cf. III, 2, 2, 34–35; VI, 8, 15, 33; VI, 8, 17, 17–18.

6. E.g., V, 3, 8, 2–5; V, 9, 9, 9; VI, 7, 5, 5–8.

7. Armstrong, in a chapter significantly entitled "The Great Logos" explains logos in Plotinus by commenting on III, 2 and 3. For him, "[These] treatises are a work of Plotinus' last period, and show a remarkable development of his thought. Their most striking feature is the appearance in them of the doctrine of Logos. This is the most extreme modification which the doctrine of the three hypostases ever undergoes in the *Enneads*" (p. 102); "The logos in these treatises appears to have taken over all the functions of the Universal Soul in relation to the sense-world" (p. 105).

These treatises (numbers 47 and 48 in the chronological order) were written within two years of Plotinus' death. In this sense they belong, no doubt, to Plotinus' "last period," but Armstrong's words suggest something more. They are within seven years, or less, of numerous treatises in which soul "retains" its "proper" place. The doctrine of logos does not suddenly "appear" in the treatises "On Providence"; it is, as the references for the present chapter indicate, spread much more widely in the *Enneads*. In III, 2, 2; III, 2, 16–18; and III, 3, 1, we find a close articulation of logos and soul. Nowhere does Plotinus represent logos as supplanting soul. It would appear that these treatises simply present, in greater detail and with a greater wealth of metaphor, a notion present throughout Plotinus' writings: that soul forms the world according to reason, that *in* its world-formation it is the vehicle of intellectuality, of logos.

For Bréhier, Plotinus is "manifestement embarrassé" when he comes to combine the doctrine of logos in III, 2 and 3 with the doctrine of the three hypostases. Bréhier nonetheless argues that logos does not, in these treatises, supplant soul ("Notice" to III, 2–3 in his edition of the *Enneads*, III, pp. 20–21). Similarly Schwyzer (*Les Sources de Plotin,* Geneva, c. 1960, p. 99), suggests that the logos of III, 2 and 3 is to be taken in a different sense from logos elsewhere in Plotinus, and ". . . dieser *logos* widersetzt sich einer Einordnung in die Hypostasentrias."

The remarks of Henry-Charles Puech and of Paul Henry (*ibid.*, p. 18) closely parallel the interpretation of logos I have given in this chapter: ". . . c'est toujours le principe de l'épanouissement" (Puech). "L'épanouissement aussi du raisonnement par rapport à l'intuition, d'une dispersion toujours plus grande par rapport à l'unité précédente, plus serrée (Henry). "Il n'y a pas toutefois chez Plotin, comme chez les Stoiciens, une tendance à tout bloquer, à centrer sa spéculation, sur la notion de Logos comme entité, comme Verbe-Raison" (Puech).

6

PLOTINUS uses the word physis ("nature") in several senses, which are necessarily, but easily, distinguished. In a general sense, nature can mean the "constitution" of a thing or a principle. This is the sense of the term in which Plotinus can refer to the nature of the body (III, 6, 6, 33–34), the nature of form (III, 6, 4, 41–43), or even the nature of the Good (VI, 8, 13, 38–40). Again, nature can mean hypostasis, as when Plotinus calls the One the first nature and the Nous the second nature.

But in *Ennead* III, 8, and in many other places, nature means the lower part of the Soul of the All. This part, functioning in plants and in the earth (for Plotinus the earth is alive) (IV, 4, 27, 11–17), is closely correlative to the generative-vegetative soul in man and animal.

Nature seems to bridge the gap between the intelligible and the visible worlds, and in nature the distinction between these two worlds might appear to be blurred. On the one hand nature is a soul (III, 8, 4, 15–16), a logos, an *eidos* (form as intelligible) (III, 8, 2, 20–23). It is immobile (*ibid.,* lines 19–22), distinct from matter and from body (cf. V, 8, 3, 1–2). Plants and animals have nature "in" them, "as it were, lying near or beside" (IV, 4, 14, 2–3). Matter does not enter into its constitution (cf. V, 9, 6, 15–20; III, 8, 2, 22–34). On the other hand there is the statement: "What comes from soul and is reflected on to matter is nature, in which, rather *before* which, real beings cease. And these are the last of the intelligible: for from these onward there are only imitations." [1]

Unless the "rather *before*" is taken in a strong sense, which does not seem warranted here, Plotinus is locating nature on the borderline between real beings and imitations (V, 1, 7, 46–48). As soul, it might be expected to be real being, but it is the last irradiation of soul towards body (IV, 4, 13, 3–5). The most enfeebled of real things, it is not exactly a real being. The contemplation which it has and is, contemplation like that of a sleeping or dreaming man, is inferior to the contemplation appropriate to a real being. Yet it is an intelligible form distinct from the visible form, which is a logos proceeding from it. [2]

Nature is not exactly real being, nor is it, without qualification, soul. It is true that Plotinus describes it as lower soul, as the offspring of soul (III, 8, 4, 15–16)—but even body, insofar as it is being, is soul. Nature is "the last of soul" (IV, 4, 13, 3–5). Soul, by descending into plants, makes another hypostasis. Thus it "seems to" descend; it descends "in a way"; there is "something of" soul, a trace of soul (V, 2, 1, 17–28), in plants. Nature is a mirror image of soul, which the soul gives to the body, (I, 1, 8, 15–23). Nature, again, is an image of the World Soul's wisdom, "possessing the last irradiated intellectuality (logos)" (IV, 4, 13, 3–5). The continuity of nature with soul is thus Plotinus' linear continuity of an inferior with a superior.

Because of the identification of contemplation with producing, Plotinus calls the product a theorema. As we have seen in chapter 4, this does not mean that the theorema is the object of contemplation, in the sense of that which is seen. Nature is not the object of soul's knowledge, yet soul "contemplates" nature. Similarly, the visible cosmos is not the object of nature's knowledge, even to the slight extent that nature has knowledge, yet nature "contemplates" the visible cosmos. The thing engendered is its theorema. It contemplates, and the lines of bodies come to be (III, 8, 4, 5–10; cf. IV, 4, 20, 22–25).

Nature is more towards the exterior than soul, and yet its contemplating-producing is still poiesis rather than praxis (III, 8, 2, 22–34; cf. III, 4, 1, 1–5). Nature does not produce in order to have something to look at, to contemplate. Men of inferior intelligence do this (cf. III, 8, 6, 31–39). Its producing is at one with its weak self-knowledge. Its product is an overflow from its quiet contemplation. It does not produce because its contemplation is weak (this, again, is characteristic of men of inferior intelligence), rather, in a manner imitating the Nous and the soul, it produces because of the vestigial strength of its contemplation. That its contemplation is weak, however, indicates that its product will be more external, more diffuse, even visible, and that the visible form, its product at one or two removes, will be "dead" and incapable of further production (cf. III, 8, 2, 30–34).

In general, Plotinus maintains the superiority of intellectual energy to mechanical energy. Even the debased intellectuality which is nature can produce better and more serenely than levers and impacts (V, 9, 6, 22–24; cf. III, 8, 2, 3–6). The doll-maker, whose work is often compared to that of nature, does not produce even the colors that he uses. Nature produces all the variety of colors and patterns (III, 8, 2, 5–9).

If *theorema* is understood to mean the product of nature's contemplation, there remains the problem of its *object*. Admitting all the qualifications necessary if we are to speak of nature's knowledge, what is it that nature sees or knows? Plotinus says that the silent contemplation in nature is directed neither above nor below (III, 8, 4, 15–18).

We might expect it to be directed above, to the soul. But we must remember that, after all, nature is a part of the soul, that nature *is* soul at a certain level. To speak of nature's contemplation is to speak of the last vestige of soul's contemplation, which is that and nothing more—a vestige, that is, of a contemplation directed toward, or rather seeking to become, Nous. Nature does not know the higher part of soul; it is rather a reflection or shadow of this higher part.

When Plotinus says that its contemplation is not directed below, he must mean that as a knowing or seeing, however humble, it is not directed towards matter.[3]

According to the line of interpretation we have been developing, the theorema of nature is its product, the sensible universe, and its object of knowledge, insofar as it has knowledge, is *itself*. Two difficulties present themselves here. First, there are expressions in *Ennead* III, 8, 4 that might suggest that the "thing engendered," the visible cosmos, is the *object* of nature's contemplation; second, and opposed to the first, there are suggestions in the same place that the theorema of nature is within nature itself.

Plotinus says that nature "sees what is after itself in such a way as is fitting to it" and so "accomplishes its theorema" (III, 8, 4, 20–22). The notion of seeing what is after itself, despite the affirmation just made that its contemplation is not directed below, is satisfactorily explained by holding that "below" refers to matter, "what is after itself" to the visible cosmos. Nevertheless, if we take the qualification "in such a way as is fitting to it" to refer only to the weakness of nature's contemplation, it would seem that the *object* of nature's vision is the sensible cosmos. But how can this be so when the contemplative producer of anything would seem to require an at least "metaphysically" prior knowledge of that which is to be produced?

If, on the other hand, the qualifying phrase is taken to mean also that nature "knows" the things of nature insofar as they exist in nature as their generator, the seeming contradictions disappear, and the context, which reaffirms the stasis and the lack of "search" on the part of nature, can be allowed its full value. The weakness of nature's contemplation is not such that it must produce objects for itself, but rather that it must produce bodies, that is, logoi "in" matter.

"Nature makes the theorema in it, which is a logos, and brings to completion another logos." (III, 8, 7, 13–14). Since Plotinus has said that the thing engendered, the visible cosmos, is nature's theorema, he must mean here that the visible cosmos is in nature in the sense that body is in the soul.[4]

Plotinus describes nature in reference both to the human soul and to the Soul of the All. We must remember that there is a soul or a part of soul in us "coming from" the Soul of the All. In the case of the human soul nature is the vegetative power below sensation and discursive reasoning, the soul which, he adds, dominates in plants because in them it is alone (III, 4, 1, 3–5). In the Soul of the All there is neither sensation nor discursive reasoning; nature, the vegetative soul in the visible cosmos, is its lowest part. The reference to plants in a context dealing primarily with nature in humans shows that the two meanings of nature are the same: vegetative soul.

The question thus arises whether sensation and discursive reasoning are higher as contemplations than nature. Sensation, we will recall, is a receiving from things. It is posterior to the sensible world. Discursive reasoning is based on sensation. Both are "searchings" rather than "havings." Further, they are occupied with external things. They are not in complete possession of their objects, since their objects are not perfectly within them (V, 3, 3, 16–18).

Nature, on the other hand, appears to have more interiority. Although nature is, as Plotinus says, "more towards the external," this first of all means more towards the external than is the higher part of the Soul of the All, and secondly, more towards the external in the sense of tending more to produce the external. The phrase does not mean that nature is "more towards the external" with regard to its object of contemplation.

The interiority of nature is involved in its being the lower part of the Soul of the All. Just as the Soul of the All is self-contained with reference to anything material, so is nature. When Plotinus speaks of the contemplation which nature has, he calls it a "*sort of synesis* and *synesthesis*" (III, 8, 5, 19–20). These expressions connote a kind of knowledge; they might even mean self-knowledge, that is, self-possession and self-knowledge, although, since they are applied to nature, obviously a debased and weakened form of self-knowledge would be implied. Therefore Plotinus seems to be describing nature as a knowing power, one which possesses its object internally, and whose object is itself. It does not search, for to search is to not yet have (III, 8, 3, 13–16; cf. III, 8, 4, 21); nature does not, like discursive reasoning, look for an object it does not yet possess. "It possesses, and for this reason, namely that it possesses, it produces" (III, 8, 3, 16–17), which is to say that it possesses itself as object of contemplation, and for this very reason it produces the sensible universe as work of contemplation.

Yet is nature, according to Plotinus, definitely superior as a contemplation to sensation and discursive reasoning? In III, 8, 5, he begins to speak of contemplation in soul, which is before nature.

Here we learn that soul is fuller than nature, is more at rest, *has more* than nature. But we find in the same sentence that soul loves learning and searches (cf. III, 8, 5, 1–6). Yet "to search is to not yet have." Nature is a contemplative producer because it *has* its object. Is soul a better contemplative producer although it does not yet have its object? Is search better, after all, than possession?

Following the line of interpretation developed in chapter 4, we might say that the soul which has more than nature is the World Soul; the soul which searches, and so has, apparently, less, is the human soul. But since Plotinus speaks here simply of soul, without explicitly indicating the distinction, the difficulty remains. It would not help to point out that the highest part of the human soul, its nous, is a contemplation superior to nature, because in the passage in question it is not this part, but the discursive part (III, 8, 5, 10–14) which is implied to be a contemplation superior to nature.

The way to a resolution may be opened by considering that it is not clear whether Plotinus intends nature's contemplation to be conscious or not. Thus sensation and discursive reasoning might be superior to nature's contemplating in the sense that, although the former do not perfectly possess their objects, they are conscious.

It may seem strange to speak of an unconscious contemplation, an unconscious knowledge. But as nature is a weak dilution of Nous "close to" matter, it could be that its contemplation is less than conscious. Twice, in fact, Plotinus seems to indicate that nature has no knowledge at all. In one place he asks, "How can the soul produce anything according to thoughts? For it is the logos in matter which produces, and that which produces in the way of nature (*physikôs*) is not thought or sight, but a power altering matter, not knowing but only acting in the manner of imprinting its figure or shape upon water . . ." (II, 3, 17, 2–5); and in another place there is the statement, "Wisdom is the first, and nature is the last . . . whence nature does not know, but only produces . . . nature does not have imagination; intellectual knowledge is better than imagination; imagination is *between* the imprint of nature and intellectual knowledge. Nature has no grasp, no synesis . . ." (IV, 4, 13, 2–14).

Nature does not know; it is only a productive power. But

according to the treatise on contemplation, nature, as a productive power, is a contemplation. Is it then a contemplation which is not knowledge? According to the treatise on contemplation, this would be impossible. Theoria and noesis have been equated. Nature "sees what is after it," and there is, explicitly, "naturely knowledge" (*phytikê noêsis*) (III, 8, 8, 14–16).

But we must recall the very limited claims that are made for nature's knowledge in III, 8. Nature has only a *sort of* synesis, a *sort of* synesthesis. Further, Plotinus says, "And if anyone wishes to accord to nature a certain synesis or perception, it is not as we speak of perception or synesis in others, but as if one were to compare the [synesis and perception] of sleep [or dream, *tou hypnou*] to those of one who is awake." (III, 8, 4, 22–25.)

Does *tou hypnou* here mean "sleep" or "dream"? We cannot be certain. Let us suppose that nature's knowing is like a dream. What would this mean? Like a dream in being uncertain or false? No, nature's knowledge is, as we have seen, a possession and not a search, therefore certain and not false. Like a dream in being vague? Some dreams are vivid, and Plotinus must have known this. Perhaps Plotinus means like a dream in being a reflection of, being dependent on and a re-play of, waking knowledge. Or perhaps he means only to indicate a type of knowledge which is, in a general way, inferior to waking knowledge. In any event we could be sure of no more than that, if "dream" is the correct word, he intends to indicate some sort of similarity between nature's contemplation and a dream. It would be an excess of romantic imagination to suppose that Plotinus means, literally, that plants and trees are dreaming.

If Plotinus says that nature's knowledge is asleep, this could mean that nature's contemplating is completely unconscious. The fact, however, that for Plotinus knowledge in the exemplar of knowledge, the Nous, is completely self-conscious and therefore completely conscious, would render unlikely the possibility that there could be, in his world, a knowledge so beclouded that it is completely unconscious. When Plotinus uses the comparison with sleep—if *hypnos* means "sleep" here—he probably wishes to convey the relative effacement of nature's knowledge. It is close to unconsciousness, close to nescience. And also, if the *anapauetai* ("is in repose," perhaps "sleeps") of the immediately succeeding sentence is to be read in connection with *tou hypnou*, he implies a comparison between nature's lack of research, the certainty and fixedness of its knowledge, and the peace of sleep.[5] In these senses, nature is *like* a man asleep: to call Plotinus' nature a "sleeping spirit" would be excessive, another bit of romantic-idealist poetry.[6]

The divergence between the statement that nature "does not know" in IV, 4 and the treatment of nature as a knower in III, 8 is, therefore, not so great as it would at first appear to be. It is reducible to a difference in emphasis. Nature is a contemplation, a knowledge, but it is a most obscure knowledge. As a knowledge, it is both better and worse than sensation and discursive reason: better in that it is a firm possession of its object; worse, in that it is more effaced.

Nature, then, is the last of the contemplative producers: the last producer that produces simply by being in possession of itself, simply by being an immobile contemplation. With nature we have reached the penultimate stage in the watering-down of the Nous' being and intellectuality. But nature is not the last reflection of Nous: that, so far as we have seen, would be the sensible cosmos itself.

NOTES

1. IV, 4, 13, 19–22. The correct interpretation of this passage hinges on the force to be accorded to the *ê*. I have taken the *ê* to be weak. It is true that Plotinus frequently uses *ê* to introduce a categorical statement of his own opinion—but this use occurs generally after a question.

2. Inge (I, 155–156) says too categorically: "Nature is the lowest of the spiritual existences. . . . Plotinus concedes reality or spiritual existence to nature."

3. In II, 4, 16, 27, matter is "what is below being."

4. There is another passage which may refer to a theorema *in* nature: "Contemplating the theorema born in it (*autê(i)*), nature rests, because it remains in itself and with itself and is [itself] a theorema." (III, 8, 4, 25–27.) It is quite possible here that *autê(i)* means *to it* (Inge renders it *of it*), in which case there is no difficulty. Nature rests in repose while contemplating (producing) its theorema—Plotinus' consistent doctrine. Or if *in it* is the correct rendering, it would mean "in" once more in the sense that body is within soul.

5. Cf. Hans-Rudolf Schwyzer, "'Bewusst' und 'Unbewusst' bei Plotin," *Les Sources de Plotin*, pp. 371–372: "Die Natur hat also eine *synesis* und *synaisthêsis*, wie sie dem Schlafenden zugebilligt werden kann, der mit sich selbst in Frieden ist."

6. "Die Natur also ist ein schlafender Geist, wie Schelling es ausgedrückt hat; sie wirkt unbewusst (*aphantastôs*)." (Arthur Christian Drews, *Plotin und der Untergang der Antiken Weltanschauung*, Jena, 1907, p. 143.) It does not seem certain that *aphantastôs* must mean, or imply, "unconsciously." It might mean "without the specific power, imagination." But did Plotinus say that nature works *aphantastôs*? Drews' footnote reference is to III, 6, 4. In that place we find (lines 18–23): "It is evident that there are two imaginations in the soul; the first, which we call opinion, and another from this, which is no longer opinion, but a sort of obscure opinion regarding the lower, and an unjudging imagination. It is like the activity in what is called nature, according to which it makes each thing, and which, *as they say*, is without imagination." (Italics mine.) This passage strongly suggests

III, 8, 1, 22–23: ". . . and [let us say] how nature, which *they say* is without imagination (*aphantastikon*) and without reason, has a contemplation in itself, and produces what it produces by the contemplation which it 'does not have'; and how . . ."

It seems plain from both III, 6, 4 and the parallel expression in III, 8, 1 that the notion that nature functions *aphantastôs* is not Plotinus' own, but another, presumably Stoic, doctrine to which he is making allusion. Cf. *Stoicorum Veterum Fragmenta*, ed. H. von Armin (Leipzig, 1903–1924), II fr. 1016; III, fr. 386.

Plotinus is not adopting the notion that nature is, in an unqualified sense, without imagination. Indeed, his meaning seems to be that nature's theoria can be regarded as a watered-down imagination, just as it is a watered-down noesis.

7

ACCORDING to the doctrine developed in the preceding chapters, the sensible world is derived from the Nous, which is true being, by the intermediation of the contemplating-producing of the Soul of the All and its lower part, nature. The sensible world is imitation being and it derives whatever reality it has from true being by the intermediation of soul.

But according to another line of reasoning in Plotinus' philosophy, intermediation by soul may not be necessary. Since matter participates directly in the intelligible world, the sensible world may be a direct product of the Nous.

For Plotinus, matter is non-being. It is not only non-being, but, in a significant phrase, it has the being of non-being (III, 6, 6, 30–32). Matter, which in its way is even a form, the last of forms (V, 8, 7, 22–23), has its own nature; but the nature of matter is to be non-being (III, 6, 6, 30–32). Matter keeps its own nature: it is what it is, and it remains what it is, because it is impassible and unchangeable.[1] "Just as, for the others, which are forms, there is no alteration according to their entity (*ousia*), for their entity consists in being unaltered, in the same way, since being (*to einai*) for matter is being as matter, that according to which matter is is not altered, but remains. As, in the previous case, the form is unalterable, so, in the latter, matter is unalterable." (III, 6, 10, 22–28.)

Matter *is* not; it is always about to be. Its being, as Plotinus says, is a reference to that which it "will" be (II, 5, 5, 3–5), but, we may add, which it will never be. Matter is a perpetual aspiration towards substance (III, 6, 7, 13), always trying to be, but never being; always trying to seize being, but always thwarted (III, 6, 14, 7–10).

Similar phrases are used to show that matter is non-good. Matter is evil even though it "participates" in the good, because it does not have the good and can never have it. It is necessarily evil (II, 4, 16, 16–21). This is not so much an attitude towards matter as a Plotinian philosophic "fact": since matter does not veritably participate in the good, it is proper to designate it as evil; since it *cannot* veritably participate in the good, it must be designated as *necessarily evil*. As absolute evil, it always tries to seize the good, but never succeeds (*ibid.*).

Since matter is being in potency, and only in potency,[2] since its nature is to be in potency, it can never be in act without ceasing altogether to be what it is.[3] Furthermore, considerations based on the production and constitution of sensible things show that matter must remain being in potency. Nothing goes away from being, in the sense that nothing is detached from the Nous-Being. There is no emanation in the sense of a literal out-flowing, involving a diminution or an alteration of the very substance of the Nous. If there were, sensible things could exist without matter, because their logoi would not have to be received into a substrate. But since no real being departs from real being, it follows that the images of real being, which are the logoi of sensible things, must be received into another—into matter. If real being appears, or appears to appear, in the visible cosmos, this receptacle, matter, is necessary. Now matter is not real being and so it cannot receive real being: it is and remains non-being. It is a seat or place prepared for being, it "strives" for being, but being does not come to it: thus it is and remains being in potency (III, 6, 14, 1–9).

Matter cannot be in act, it cannot unite with form: it cannot be formed (II, 5, 5, 21–22). Significantly, Plotinus speaks in several places of the form *on* matter (*epi hylê(i)*) rather than *in* matter (*en hylê(i)*) (II, 4, 8, 23–25; V, 9, 2, 13–14). His interpretation of *Timaeus* 52a, in III, 6, 12, 1–6, expresses his own doctrine: "Plato thinks this [the foregoing, i.e., that matter is impassible] about matter, and that the participation does not consist in a form (*eidos*) becoming, as though in a substrate, and giving the substrate a form (*morphê*), so that one composite should come to be, made up of [the two] turning together and, as it were, mixing together, and suffering from each other. He wishes to establish that this is not his meaning, and to show how matter, while remaining impassible, possesses the forms (*eidê*) . . ." The impassibility of matter rules out any true union between matter and form in Plotinus' sensible world.

Yet certain of Plotinus' statements about matter appear to contradict this view. He says that matter is always ordered, that it was never not ordered (IV, 3, 9, 17); form leaves no matter unformed (VI, 7, 3, 10–11). Again, "We posited . . . that when form comes upon matter, matter [from being], as it were, a dream of the good, has come to be on a higher level." (VI, 7, 28, 7–12.) Further, Plotinus says that sensible matter, presumably under the influence of form, "*becomes something determinate or limited,* not indeed living or intelligent, but a dead thing which is ordered." (II, 4, 5, 17. Italics mine.)

In view of what has been said above, these can be no more than expressions, from the point of view of matter, of matter's attempt to "seize" form. Matter is ordered, is formed, becomes on a higher level, becomes something definite, *insofar as it can,* which is really not at all: "The being (*to einai*) of matter is not injured by that which gives it form; it does not run a risk, because of the giving of form, of being less evil, because it always remains that which it is." (III, 6, 11, 39–41.)

Plotinus compares matter to a mirror, and the "beings" which are "in" it to the images in a mirror.[4] It is an analogy which excellently illustrates Plotinus' whole doctrine of matter and sensible things. If the things we see in a mirror were really there, then it could also be true that real beings would be present in matter (III, 6, 13, 49–51), but of course what is reflected in a mirror is not really present there. A mirror seems to possess everything, but actually possesses nothing (III, 6, 7, 26–27). No more than the image in a mirror affects the mirror[5] do the reflections or images of real being *upon* matter affect matter (III, 6, 11, 15–18; 36–41). Further, the mirror which is matter is non-being, so that the visible cosmos is, as it were, a reflection which is non-being in a mirror which is non-being. The sensible world is a phantom in a phantom.[6] Both matter and the sensible world have the "being of non-being": "It is necessary that body is not, and the substrate of body is not: their being is the being of things which are not."[7]

The sensible world is non-being, but Plotinus does not despise it. The sensible world is beautiful (V, 8, 8, 7–23). To criticize it, as the Gnostics do, is to expect it to be the intelligible world—this is foolish, it is only an imitation. "But what other image of the intelligible world could be more beautiful than this? What other fire, besides the fire in the sensible world, is a better image of the intelligible fire? Or what other earth than the sensible earth? Is there a more perfect sphere, one more venerable, or one more regular in its movement, except the compass of the intelligible cosmos itself? What other sun is there, better than the visible sun, except the sun of the intelligible world?"[8] In this, as in other passages, the sensible world is seen as a reproduction of the intelligible world. The plants in the intelligible world are the paradigms of the plants "here" (VI, 7, 11, 6–17; cf. Timaeus 30c–d).

Yet the "forms" which are seen in the sensible world are a lie; matter is a lie (III, 6, 7, 40–41); the sensible world is a lie. Plotinus can even say that the images of forms which appear on matter have no similarity to the true beings (ibid., lines 33–40). His point is that the sensible is a lie if it is mistaken for the intelligible. In this way, the best possible image is a lying image. The "forms" in the sensible world have no similarity to the true beings precisely because they are non-being.

Plotinus is not saying that there is no being in the sensible world—the intelligible world is the being of the sensible world, but that there is no being in it qua sensible. On this point he is explicating Plato brilliantly. In the order of true knowledge the lying images of the senses are nothing and tell us nothing. As we begin to become Nous, as the world begins to become intelligible for us, the world begins to be seen as what it is: the intelligible world.

The comparison of matter to a mirror has been useful to Plotinus. But he sees it is in need of correction. Matter "mirrors" true being; but not only is it a mirror which is itself non-being, not only is there a radical dissimilarity between the reflected and the reflection, but there is no spatial separation of this "mirror" and the reflections upon it from real being.

The intelligible universe is neither far from nor near to the visible universe (VI, 4, 2, 48). That is, the notions of spatial separation and contiguity, which have relevance only within the visible universe, are inapplicable here. Spatial notions can be applied only metaphorically. Granted this, it can be said that the visible universe is *in* the intelligible,[9] as the body is in the soul (IV, 3, 20, 46–51), the "less" in the "greater" (VI, 4, 2, 30–34): "Then, if there is established in the intelligible All something else which is 'beside' it, this [the visible All] participates in it, and happens together with it and derives its power from it. The visible All does not partition the intelligible, but finds itself in the intelligible All because it comes from the intelligible All: while the intelligible All does not come to be outside of itself. For it is not possible for being to be in non-being, but rather non-being is in being." (VI, 4, 2, 17–22.)

Clearly, Plotinus does not mean here that the intelligible All is a *place* containing the visible All (cf. *ibid.*, lines 6–11). The visible All is "in" the intelligible as the derived strength is in its source of strength, or better, since the images in matter are actually without force (III, 6, 7, 28–31; III, 8, 2, 30–32), as the powerless is in the powerful; or again, as the produced is in the producer.

The notion bears a similarity to the conception of Christian philosophy that the universe is in God.[10] But since the visible universe for Plotinus is non-being, there is, to his way of thinking, all the stronger reason why it must be "in" the intelligible universe. Paradoxically: since it has no being, no strength, no truth, it can in no sense be "outside" of being, power, and truth: because whatever it has (and ontically it has nothing) must be in complete dependence upon being, it can have no separate existence—it is in no sense "on its own."

Plotinus employs still another spatial metaphor, that of *presence*. The intelligible world is present to the sensible world—and yet again not present, since the intelligible world remains by itself (*eph' heautou*), even when something tries to be present to it (VI, 4, 2, 37–39). The incommensurability of being and non-being, of the intelligible world and the visible world, makes it impossible for one properly to be present to another. But as the visible is the immediate image of the intelligible, it would be similarly improper to say that they are distant from one another.

The foregoing themes—matter, the impassible, unaffected by form; matter, the mirror, reflecting true being; the visible All, the reflection of being on matter, as neither near to nor far from the intelligible All; the "presence" of the visible All to the intelligible— express more or less metaphorically what Plotinus formulates most theoretically as the "participation of matter in the intelligible world" (cf. *Timaeus*, 61a–b).

"Participation" is the contact of matter to the intelligible world, by which matter receives what it can receive.[11] But matter "participates, and does not participate, in the intelligible world" (VI, 4, 8, 41–42), because by this "participation" the intelligible world is not dissipated, and matter is not affected. This follows from all that has been said so far in this chapter. Matter is impassible; it cannot change. Participation is not, then, a passion for matter. The mode of participation leaves matter intact, non-being, evil; leaves it purely and always being in potency (III, 6, 11, 15–41).

Yet matter participates in the intelligible world; further, each thing in the sensible universe participates in the *whole* of the intelligible universe (VI, 4, 12, 41–49). Plotinus' thought is that the intelligible universe itself cannot be partitioned (VI, 4, 2, 17–22). We remember that it is the one-many, more perfectly united than the sensible universe, since it is more perfectly united than the soul of the sensible universe, which is one *and* many.

That the intelligible universe cannot be partitioned would seem to mean that it is not divided into parts, one part of which is reflected by one part of matter to give, for example, the image of tree, and another part reflected by another part of matter to give the image of horse. Rather, apparently, any matter, any part of matter—if we can speak of parts of matter—reflects the whole of the intelligible universe insofar as it is able (cf. *ibid.*, lines 46–49).

Matter thus appears to participate *directly* in the intelligible world. Matter is, as it were, touching the idea from all sides and yet not touching it. There is nothing in between matter and the idea (VI, 5, 8, 15–21). It would seem that there is no room for the intermediation effected by soul and nature.

NOTES

1. III, 6, 9, *passim;* III, 6, 11, 29–31; III, 6, 14, 29; III, 6, 15, 6–10.

2. II, 5, 5, 1–4; cf. II, 5, 4, 4: Matter is all beings in potency.

3. II, 5, 5, 27–36. In view of Plotinus' consistent doctrine of the immutability of matter it is impossible to accept Inge's statement (I, 127) that "In the Sixth Ennead he [Plotinus] objects that the Stoic doctrine gives the first place to that which is only potential (*dynamei*), whereas the possibility of passing into activity and actuality (*energeia*) is the only thing that makes Matter respectable. . . . Matter cannot improve itself; it can only pass into activity by the help of what is above and before it." One must assume that Inge intends "can" to connote a realizable potency, since he contrasts it with *dynamei,* "only potential." But Inge's reference is to VI, 1, 26, where Plotinus uses only the word *dynamei* and does not say that matter is realizably able to or ever does "pass into activity and actuality."

4. The basic comparison is made in III, 6, 7, 22–33: ". . . and the being which matter has in fantasy is non-being, as a fugitive toy: whence those things that seem to become in it are toys, really phantoms in a phantom, as in a mirror, in which a thing appears to be in a different place from that in which it is. The mirror seems to be full: it possesses nothing, and it seems to possess everything. What enters into and goes out of matter is the imitations of beings, and images going in and out of a formless image. Because it is formless the things which are seen in it seem to act with regard to it, but they effect nothing: they are feeble and weak, they have no solidity. Nor does matter have any solidity. They go through matter without dividing it, as images go through water, or as if someone were to send forms into what has been called the void."

5. Plotinus calls matter "less passible than a mirror" (III, 6, 9, 16–19). He may consider that a mirror is affected in some way by the things which are reflected in it. In III, 6, 7, 33–43, he may imply that in those cases where there is a similarity between the reflected and the reflection, a certain power of the reflected thing affects the reflecting body.

6. III, 6, 7, 24. The expression *eidôla en eidôlô(i)* could have the weaker meaning "an image in an image" but it occurs in the place where Plotinus has just said that the being that seems to be in matter is a "fugitive toy."

7. III, 6, 6, 30–32. This answers those (the Stoics) who "would place being in bodies." *Ibid.,* lines 65 ff.

8. II, 9, 4, 22–32. It is possible that over the years Plotinus' expressed "attitude" towards the sensible world underwent a change from "pessimism" to "optimism," as he lost hope of "converting" his Gnostic pupils (cf. *Les Sources de Plotin,* pp. 182–185, remarks of M. Puech). But his philosophic point seems always to have been the same: There is nothing wrong with the sensible world, so long as it is not mistaken for the intelligible world (*vide infra,* chapter 8).

9. We should recall that, following his other line of argument, Plotinus also says that the visible universe is in the Soul of the All (V, 5, 9, 27–32).

10. E.g., St. Thomas Aquinas, *Summa Theologiae,* I, 8, 1, ad 2.

11. Plotinus says in VI, 5, 8, 1–22, which introduces "contact," that he is speaking "more accurately"; he is no longer using the images of radiation and mirroring. For this reason the doctrine of the participation of matter in the ideas is "most difficult." But clearly, in using the notion of contact, Plotinus does not fully escape from sensible images—to do so is an impossibility for any philosopher. The word "participation" itself has, radically, a sensible meaning.

8

THE CLOSELY textual presentation of Plotinus' treatments of contemplation and production, in which the sensible world has been seen as the product of Nous and/or nature contemplating, must be supplemented by an attempt to understand more profoundly the import of what Plotinus is saying.

If we wish to treat Plotinus as merely an historical curiosity, it is enough for us to repeat what he himself has said in somewhat similar language, bringing together the texts from various places and letting them stand on their own. If, however, we wish to take him seriously as a philosopher, as someone who can speak to us intelligently and enlighteningly about the world in which we live and with which we are confronted, we must go a step further and try to "make sense" of his account for ourselves. And that means we must find our way from the world we experience in our non-philosophical moments to the world as it is described in the *Enneads;* we must find an illumination of our world in his account. Otherwise, his dicta remain for us so many "interesting" statements that bear little or no relation to the world we want to understand philosophically.

With Plotinus, finding that way has its own particular difficulties. For when he tells us that "nature" is a "contemplation" and that contemplation is what "produces" the sensible universe, he seems far from describing the everyday world; he seems, at best, to have got everything upside down. In this and the following chapter I wish to show that this impression is mistaken.

The "nature" that Plotinus is treating is, according to his own account, the nature in plants, that is, the nature in growing things. Now, what Plotinus knows about trees and about plants generally is what anyone knows. He knows that plants grow, that they produce seeds. He knows that, to common observation, plants are living, and material things below the level of plants are non-living (cf. VI, 7, 15, 16–21). He knows that all material things, including plants, are extended, separate from one another, and impinging upon one another. In general, it would seem that Plotinus senses the material world as we do, and that his uncriticized, pre-philosophic intellectual conception of this world is basically the same as anyone else's.

Does this mean that Plotinus considered the sensible universe to be real? "Real" is not a Plotinian term. Plotinus does speak of "being," by which he means the veritable being in the Nous; if we consider "real" as an adjective co-ordinate with "being," the answer to the above question is at once "no." In the technical Plotinian sense the sensible universe as sensible is non-being. But our present question is not answered this easily, because we are not asking whether the sensible universe is "being" for Plotinus, but whether it is real for him. If we distinguish, therefore, Plotinus' naive, original view of trees and plants from his philosophic evaluation of them, it is clear that since his everyday world is the same as ours, trees and plants are real for him. They are observable. They may be technically "non-being," but they are never called "non-existent." They are not unreal, nor fictitious, nor, pre-philosophically at any rate, mental or ideal.

But when Plotinus says, philosophically, that the nature of plants and trees is a contemplation, is he not making them out to be less than real? Is not "thought" less real than "things"?

The objection that thought is not as real as things probably means nothing more than that human thought is less real than material things. Now the contemplation which, for Plotinus, is nature (*a*) is not thought, (*b*) is not human, (*c*) is for him more real than material things. Let us examine these points one by one.

First of all, for Plotinus as for Aristotle, any contemplation is knowledge (*vide* Appendix II). Plotinus does not view it as consideration, or mulling over. For this reason it is a mistake to take "contemplation," as he uses it, to be "thought," if by "thought" we mean a mental process or act which is not in firm possession of its object. The contemplation which is nature is an obscure knowledge, indefinite in the sense of being not fully aware, perhaps not aware at all, but not indefinite in the sense of not being in possession of its object. Nature does not reason, or seek knowledge; nature has knowledge, it *is* a knowledge.

But nature is not an act of human cognition. The properly human cognitive act is, for Plotinus, discursive reasoning, what he calls logismos or dianoia (cf. V, 3, 3, 31–39). In discursive reasoning, the object is not yet possessed, it is being sought. Thus discursive reasoning is not yet knowledge. Since Plotinus holds that nature is always in firm, though obscure, possession of its object of knowledge, he cannot mean that it is an act of properly human cognition.

For the same reason nature cannot very well be a figment of, or a projection of, human discursive reasoning. Similarly it cannot be an act of, or a figment of, or a projection of, sensation. For Plotinus, as for almost any philosopher, sensation is not from the outset in possession of its object. Sensation, like discursive reasoning, involves a seeking and a reception.

Plotinus, rather, thinks of nature as being, in itself and in its own way, an obscure act of knowing. Its relation to sensation and to discursive reasoning seems to be that it can be an object for these human cognitive functions.

Plotinus takes the contemplation which for him is nature to be real—more real than material things. This does not mean that material things are less than real, but rather that whatever makes them real is possessed in a higher fashion by contemplative nature.

What do we mean by "real" in the present connection? Something like this: The same "quality" which anyone finds in material things, present in something which might be regarded as ghostly, ephemeral, epiphenomenal. We might say that Plotinus' psychological reaction to contemplation is similar to our reaction to something solid, something "substantial" in the proper sense. Contemplation is, for Plotinus at least, what we would call a "thing."

But as we have seen, contemplation is knowledge, and therefore the reality of contemplation is the reality of knowledge. The point, then, is that Plotinus took knowledge to be real, more real than "things." How is the reader likely to understand this? Perhaps that Plotinus was introverted, lost in his own thoughts, which in time he believed more "substantial" than the real world around him. Plotinus, it is true, was an intellectual's intellectual, very much aware of the value and "solidity" of knowledge. He regarded no knowledge as ghostly or ephemeral. But it would be idle to pretend to say to what extent this disposition of his influenced his ultimate philosophy—there would be practically no evidence to support any conclusion. As a matter of fact, it is probable that the disposition itself is consequent upon the philosophy. He presents well-reasoned arguments which show that knowledge is more real than sensible, material things—these are more worthy of consideration than would be his dispositions.

But the knowledge which for him is more real than material things is not properly human knowledge, and it is not, primarily, the knowledge which is contemplative nature; rather it is superior to both. For Plotinus, there is a world of true being, "above" (to speak metaphorically) the sensible, material world which is the world of imitation being; that is to say, for him there is a more real world "above" this real world. Now the more real world, the world of true being, is identical with true knowledge. True knowledge, the knowledge which is most real, is the knowledge possessed by the Nous, often called the "divine intellect." It is the knowledge which is true being.

Let us, as Plotinus himself does, give a crude description of the world of true being, which can be refined subsequently. The world of true being appears to duplicate the sensible world (vide supra, p. 96). There are trees, plants, earth, etc., in the world of true being. There are, however, these differences between the world of true being and the material, sensible world: everything in the world of true being is eternal and immutable, and everything is identical with knowledge of itself. For example, the tree in the world of true being is identical with the knowledge of tree.

Why must there be a true-being tree? Why must there be a more real tree? Is Plotinus despairing of explaining the real world, and taking refuge in a heaven of ideas? And, even supposing for a time that there is a tree in a world of true being, why must it be identical with knowledge of tree?

Plotinus' answer to this question would comprise the following two points: (a) the tree in the world of true being *is* tree, that is to say, it is self-identical. It is true being, true tree because it is self-identical. And (b) identity with knowledge is necessary for self-identity, or, more properly, self-identity *is*, exactly, knowledge of self. Let us discuss both arguments.

The "beingly" tree is self-identical. This is comprehensible, but seems tautological. A thing *is* when it is itself. "Of course," one might say, "but is not the sensible tree also itself? When is a thing ever not itself?" There would seem nevertheless to be cases in which a thing is not itself. A tree in a dream, or a tree in a mirror, is not a tree. Plotinus uses precisely these instances to illustrate his meaning. For him, the sensible tree is like a tree in a dream or a tree in a mirror—not, however, in the sense of being unreal, but in the sense of not being identical with tree.

This is why Plotinus says that the nature in a sensible tree is like a dream. It is *like* a dream, but it is not one of our dreams. It is a reality which is like a dream when compared to something which is more real. Similarly the nature or form of the sensible tree is like a reflection in a mirror. Not that it *is* a reflection in a mirror, but that it is a reality which, as compared to a "higher" reality, is like a mirror reflection thereof.

Still, why is the sensible tree not "tree-itself"? Principally because (and this brings us to the second part of the argument delineated above) an entity such as a tree is properly itself only when it is identical with knowledge of itself. A thing is itself when it has a grasp of itself, when it has possession of itself, when it is interior to itself, when it is transparent to itself. These conditions are realized only in self-knowledge.

The same result can be reached by starting with cognition rather than with things. Plotinus is perfectly aware that ordinary human cognition is not identical with its object. But what is cognition trying to accomplish? For Plotinus, it is seeking full possession of its object, that is, it is trying to *be* its object. The cognition which *is* its object is the only cognition which is, properly speaking, knowledge.

The object, on the other hand, if it is to be "being," must be knowledge. Therefore Plotinus sees in the ordinary dualism of cognition and object an urge toward, and a reflection of, knowledge-being or being-knowledge.

Further, Plotinus knows that knowledge tends to unity, that the parts of knowledge are in communication, interconnection. Conversely, he knows that the sensible world itself tends to unity, that its parts are interconnected and harmonized, albeit imperfectly.

The knowledge-being, then, which is "above" both ordinary cognition and the sensible universe is a perfect intercommunication. It is both all knowledges and all beings and also Knowledge and Being. Knowledge-Being is the Nous. The ordinary translation, "Intellect," is perhaps remote; we could remain close to the etymology in rendering it the "Knower."

But someone might argue: "Granted that the urge of being is towards self-identity through self-knowledge, and that the urge of knowledge is towards identification with being, what proof do we have that these identities, which are really one identity, are actually achieved? How do we know that there is a world of true being? How do we know that there is a Knower which is this world of true being?"

On this subject Plotinus often speaks with the sureness of experience. The "Knower" is not exactly human intellect, because intellect, for Plotinus, is never, technically speaking, human, but more than human. Yet it is the intellect which a man has or is when he is at the level of intellectual knowledge (V, 3, 3, 21–29). Now Plotinus sometimes speaks as though he himself had attained this level, as though he had been the Knower.[1]

But is not the Knower, the Nous, divine intellect? When Plotinus describes the world of true being as though he existed in that world, is he not indulging in "mysticism"? Can we follow him at all in the experience of being the Knower?

At this point, we may wonder about the designation of the Nous as "divine intellect." Plotinus surely calls it divine, but Greek philosophers (and poets) used "divine" in a very extensive sense. When a Christian, or someone influenced by Christianity, hears the phrase "divine intellect" he supposes that it means the intellect of God, the intellect in God. Plotinus' God is the One. The Nous, the Knower, is not the intellect in the One; there is, at least technically, no intellect in the One. The Nous is definitely below the One; it is caused by the One. An intellect caused by the One and below the One is not, in a Christianized vocabulary, a divine intellect.

Granted that the Knower is not divine intellect as we would understand it, and granted that Plotinus at times *is* the Knower, still Plotinus realizes that the Knower is not easily accessible to man, even to a philosopher. Often it is more a case of describing the Nous as it were from the outside. Plotinus sees that sensible things do not achieve identity with knowledge; he sees that ordinary human cognition does not achieve identity with its object. He seems to argue from the tendency of things to self-identity, and the tendency of cognition to identity with its object, to a Knower which is *Being*.

What, in sum, is the Knower? Is it the "ideal of intellectual knowledge," something towards which intellectual knowledge is striving but which is, at present, unreal? This is not at all the way the Knower looks to Plotinus. For him, the Knower *is*, it exists, it is living, it is eternal, it is more real than the efforts made to reach it. Further, it is not what intellectual knowledge seeks to become, or to be like: there is no intellectual knowledge which is not the Knower's knowledge, or, to put it another way, cognition is not knowledge unless it is the Knower's knowledge. *To the extent that* his cognition is knowledge a man *is* the Knower.

We have described the Knower or Nous at length because the knowledge, the contemplation which is more real than things, is properly the knowledge possessed by the Nous. We have seen that this contemplation is identified with being, that is, with the more real, and, in fact, with the being even of such things as trees.

In the Nous, in the world of true being, the being of tree is a fully self-conscious contemplation. Nature is a declination from true being and from fully self-conscious contemplation. Yet in nature the identity of "being" and "knowing" is still relatively preserved, although the "being" is imitation being, the knowledge is as in a dream or a sleep, and the identity is relaxed.

The nature of sensible, material things, is both real *and* an act of contemplation because the Nous which is more real is, just because it is more real, necessarily an act of contemplation. Nature, a declination from the Nous, preserves, in a complexly diminished fashion, the character of the Nous as knowledge-being.

Still remaining within the context of a crude description, in which the Knower, which is true being, is a world "above" the sensible world, a context in which nature is seen as a declination from the Nous, the sensible world can be explained as in some way composed of nature and matter. We have seen in a preliminary fashion that nature is real for Plotinus, although there is something more real: now, to further our understanding of the reality of nature, we will see whether matter is real for him.

Plotinus' notion of matter is from the outset philosophic. The matter of which he speaks is not matter as we might initially understand the word. It is not the "stuff" of which material things are constituted, nor is it matter as "material things" or "material thing." What we might consider the materiality of the sensible universe, Plotinus would call simply *bulk*. Now for him, matter is not bulk, rather it is the component in the sensible universe which makes it not to be the intelligible universe. Plotinus looks from the top down. He himself has functioned as Nous, or at least he has come to see the requirements of Nous, and as a consequence he knows that the world of everyday experience is not the world of true being, the intelligible universe. Why not? Because in the sensible universe the world of being is contained in a receptacle, mirrored in a mirror which is not being. This mirror is matter.

At this point, he might easily be mistaken to mean that the sensible universe mirrors, that is, imitates, an "ideal" world. But as we have already seen, his world of being is far other than an "ideal" world. Furthermore, his doctrine is not that the sensible world mirrors the world of being, but that *matter* mirrors the world of being.

Mirror is only a metaphor—a metaphor which will help us to understand Plotinus' meaning but which must be abandoned ultimately. At the outset, it conveys Plotinus' meaning very well Matter is a mirror, a mirror *as* a mirror, a mirror solely in its function of mirroring. Plotinus' matter is not a physical mirror which reflects other physical things. It is pure reflecting quality, pure reflector. Nevertheless it is not, as a modern commentator might be inclined to suppose, a notion or concept of matter.[2] To take it this way would be to idealize and so to falsify Plotinus. His point is not that the world of being is reflected in a concept of matter, but that it is reflected in matter. Likewise matter is not an abstraction. For Plotinus it would be real as opposed to ideal, its existence guaranteed by the fact that the sensible universe is not the world of being.

The matter which reflects being is other than being: it is non-being. This does not, as we have observed in other connections, mean non-existent or unreal. Matter is non-being in the sense that it is not form, not order, not knowledge.[3] As a mirror it reflects the world of true being, the world of Nous. In the simple language which Plotinus himself sometimes employs, the world of true being contains the veritable tree. The sensible tree is a reflection of the veritable tree upon matter, or, more accurately, the form, the nature of tree which is upon matter is a reflection. Does this mean that for Plotinus the nature of tree is not really present in the trees which we, and he, experience? Is he making the visible, observable world unreal after all? To escape being misled by such questions we should recall that the whole comparison of matter to a mirror is just that—a comparison. Just as pools of water mirror the sensible world, so matter mirrors the world of true being. Plotinus can hold this without detracting in the least from the reality of matter or of the sensible world. That he is not dissolving the palpable, bulky world of everyday experience in the elusive unreality of mirror images and dreams is evidenced precisely by his comparing the sensible world to mirror images. In doing so he recognizes that the sensible world has its own imitations (dreams and mirror-images). He is not saying that the sensible world is an imitation of itself, but rather that it is an imitation of the higher, more real world of true being.

But we may concede all this, and still wonder whether, for Plotinus, the sensible tree is a tree or not. If it is not, it would seem that his whole elaborate structure collapses. The question, indeed, seems to be pre-judged. Has not Plotinus held that a tree is, properly speaking, the true-being tree in the world of true being, and that the sensible tree, since it is not identical with this, is not a tree? More precisely, Plotinus' doctrine is that the sensible tree is not *self*-identical. But surely this appears paradoxical. The sensible tree is, it would seem clear, the sensible tree. But is it? What, indeed, is the sensible tree? Not merely a sensible tree, that is, a tree as accessible to sense, but a tree as accessible to any non-falsifying knowing power whatever. As a matter of fact, as common sense probably does not know, but as most philosophers, whatever their philosophies, do, tree is not known precisely by sense. Tree, if there is any such, and if it can be known, can be known only by another power, which is usually called intellect.

Now Plotinus would agree that the sensible tree is a tree. He would interpret this as meaning that the physical tree which we observe is, as known by intellect, tree. This is to say that the sensible tree, *insofar as it is a tree*, is the true-being tree, the veritable tree in the world of true being.

Thus, for Plotinus, "the sensible tree is the sensible tree" could be admitted as a fruitless tautology. As providing any insight into what the sensible tree *is*, it would be useless. The amended statement, "The sensible tree is tree," tells what the sensible tree veritably *is*, yet it is untrue of the sensible tree precisely as sensible. In other words, Plotinus' meaning is that the sensible tree as sensible is non-identical with its own being.

But if the sensible tree, as known by intellect, by the power which can know what things are, is the tree which has true being, this indicates that Plotinus does not have two worlds, but only one. His world of true being is not, except metaphorically, a world above the everyday world. It *is* the everyday world, not as experienced by sense, by opinion, or by discursive reasoning, but as known by intellect, the Nous, the Knower.

Plotinus' world of true being is, therefore, the real world of everyday experience when the latter is known by the best knowing power. The more real turns out to be in the real, in fact, to be the reality of the real. Being, which seemed at one time to be for Plotinus a technical term less extensive than reality, seems able now to coincide with reality, as common sense would appear to demand.

But is such a resolution satisfactory? The reader might object: "This man is telling us that the world of everyday experience would, if subjected to some mysterious knowing power, turn out to be not at all the way we think it is. Plotinus would have us believe that our ordinary observations and opinions about the world are untrue, but that to some inner eye the world is what it does not in any way appear to be, that is, knowledge."

It must be admitted that Plotinus does toy with the notion that sensation and opinion are false. At times he seems willing to grant skeptical arguments challenging their validity (cf. V, 5, 1, 12–15). But this is not his proper point. For the actual purposes of his own philosophy, he has nothing against sensation or opinion provided that they are not mistaken for intellectual knowledge. What we experience by our senses—colors, shapes, the hard and the soft, etc.—are real, but they are not the being of the things in which they really exist.

Sensation and opinion, if handled properly, are not taken as knowledge of the world as it is, but, in the technical sense of "is," of what it is not. By them, we experience the non-being features of the sensible world—not, it should be noted, matter, which is known only by intellect, and then by a spurious, an indirect knowledge—but rather the features of the sensible world that come about from its being a reflection of being upon non-being.

The reader who does not follow Plotinus here has, quite possibly, philosophized the so-called sense qualities as so many entities. He will suppose, then, that Plotinus is opposing these sensible entities to other entities accessible to intellect, to the denigration of the former. Plotinus' argument would be that the only entity in the sensible thing is the intelligible entity.

The point is not simply that the sensible universe contains both being and non-being, and that both are real. This is true in a loose sense, but more properly the being contains the non-being. The sensible non-being is real not because it is an entity alongside of the being, but because it is contained in the being.

Plotinus can maintain, then, that trees and plants, both as true being and as imitation being—that is, both as Nous and as nature—contemplate and are contemplations. Nature as such is both fully real *and* an act of knowing, a contemplation.

NOTES

1. Cf., e.g., V, 3, 6, 12–18; VI, 5, 7, 1–8.

2. Cf., e.g., Pistorius, p. 3: "For Plotinus it [matter] is merely a logical abstraction"; *ibid.* p. 119: "Matter does not exist. It is the logical abstraction of Negation-Absolute." Inge, I, 128: "It is a mere abstraction."

3. "It remains, then, that if [evil, i.e., matter] is, it is in those things which are not, as a sort of form of non-being. It is connected with (*peri*) something which is mixed with non-being, or has some sort of community with non-being. It is not altogether non-being; it is only other than being: not as the movement and rest connected with being are non-being, but as an image of being, or rather still more non-being [than is an image of being]." (I, 8, 3, 3–9.)

9

PLOTINUS' doctrine of nature as contemplation is intended, as we have seen, as an account of production. By contemplating, nature *makes* the things of the visible world. But to say that contemplation is productive will seem paradoxical. Suppose we grant that contemplation is not daydreaming, or "thinking," but knowing. Still, is it not impractical, useless knowledge: the pointless mulling over of something already known? How could this interior, this "mental" activity *make* anything? Is not making accomplished only by the action of one solid material thing on another solid material thing? The men on the assembly line make, produce, the automobile. They use tools, they exert physical force. Carpenters and masons build a house with their hands. Structural steel workers build a bridge.

Does Plotinus, for whom making and contemplating are apparently one and the same, have any appreciation of what carpenters and masons actually do and must do? Or is he like the occultists who believe in "mind over matter," perhaps like those who say that they can make a plant grow just by thinking at it? Does he live exclusively in a world of dreams or ideas in which thought is spontaneously productive? Or if the work of actual physical producers *is* real for him, how can he maintain that contemplation is productive?

Let us take a closer look at making. It is not only the riveters who build a bridge. The governmental body that commissions the building, the contractors, the engineers—each of these groups "build" the bridge. None of them functions directly as a material agent bringing physical force to bear on a physical thing to be modified. An engineer "builds" a bridge, and yet what he contributes to it is his knowledge and his thought. Similarly, if a man builds something which he himself has planned, he translates his own thought into action. Thought, in cases such as these, affects material things, so that, understood in this way, the action of "mind" upon matter is not at all mysterious; it is an everyday occurrence.

But thought does not appear to be *immediately* productive. The engineer must transmit his thought, directly or indirectly, to the workmen. They, in turn, must use their hands and tools—physical instruments to bring about a physical effect. The man who works according to his own plans must make a "special resolve" to act, and he too must use hands and tools. He cannot build a chair by thinking about chairs, not even by thinking about building chairs.

It might seem that unless and until thoughts and plans are translated into action they are hazy, ephemeral, impractical—not real, or at least not as real as the physical effects which they may, in time, accomplish. Nevertheless, when engineers, architects, planners in general, whose contribution to the effect is a contribution of thought and knowledge, are recognized as builders, we may with justice ask the question, "Who are the builders in the higher sense of the term: the planners, or the workmen?" Is there not a sense in which thought and knowledge are more a cause of a bridge, or an automobile, than are the actions of those who physically construct the bridge and the automobile? Yet it would still appear that, though in certain circumstances thought and knowledge are productive of physical effects, nevertheless they are insufficient of themselves to accomplish these effects.

Now Plotinus is quite aware that men make things. There is no suggestion in his writing that the physical making done by any man is unreal. For him, as for anyone, to cite the instances he himself mentions, the painter paints the picture, the sculptor makes the statue, doll-makers make dolls, architects build houses.[1] The more stupid children who are, in his words, "reduced to crafts and works" surely make things.

When Plotinus speaks of, or alludes to, ordinary making, which he calls "praxis," he shows that he is quite aware of its nature and vicissitudes. Not at all does he suppose that it is an easy imposition of "mind" upon "matter" or that it is accomplished by "mere thought."

In the case of praxis, as Plotinus describes it, the maker's "knowledge," actually sensation, opinion, and discursive reasoning, is derived, through learning, from the sensible world. His "knowledge" is subject to the requirements of the sensible world. The maker is not sure how his productive activity will turn out in the material world. He acts on imperfect knowledge, and his action can suffer from the interference of other causes. He must plan; he must readjust his plans. His making is "intelligent" in a loose sense, but not in Plotinus' technical meaning, because his making does not flow from true knowledge, such as is possessed by the Nous. Such a maker, a man of praxis, must seek to produce; he must "resolve" to produce. He must act, either directly or through others, in the physical universe in a physical way, producing sensible things by sensible means. He uses hands, levers, tools. He is obviously a maker.

For Plotinus there is, however, another and better way in which knowledge—in this case knowledge in the proper sense of the word—can bring about results in the sensible world. It is the "automatic" producing of sensible things by the contemplations which are Nous and nature. He vigorously combats the notion that praxis, with the limitations that it implies, is the pattern of all "intelligent" making. He envisages a type of knowledge which flows immediately into action, or better, is immediately productive. The Nous simply contemplates, and soul and the physical universe are produced. Nature simply contemplates, and the things of nature come to be. Nous and nature, as contemplators, produce the sensible world without learning, without seeking, without resolve, without hands, tools, or instruments.

Where is the evidence that there is such a mode of intelligent production, so different from the modes ordinarily apprehended? For Plotinus, the primary evidence is in an intellectual understanding of the world. What makes a sensible tree a tree to the extent that it is a tree? What causes it, as sensible, to be an imitation tree? What causes it to go through the changes which enable it to become, insofar as it can, more a tree? To all these questions he would answer: What it ontically is, the true-being tree. Now this true-being tree is, as we have seen in the last chapter, identical with knowledge of tree. In other words, when the world is looked at by intellect, it is seen that knowledge in the proper sense of the word, the knowledge which is identical with true being, is productive.

The sensible things have their reality by imitating the true beings. Any actions the sensible things perform, any changes they undergo—and they are constantly changing—happen because they are imitating, insofar as they can, the true beings (cf. III, 7, 11, 56–59). That is to say, all results in the sensible world come about because of the true beings. When it is accepted that the process of ordering and forming that takes place in the sensible world is a reflection of being-knowledge from the world of true being, it becomes clear that knowledge, contemplation, as it exists in the Nous, is a more powerful and a more real maker than is the man of praxis who produces things in the sensible world.

Similarly, nature, on its own level, produces the things of the sensible world. Like Nous, nature does not know the sensible world by a knowledge derived from that world. Nor does it produce the sensible world by such a knowledge, but by a prior knowledge. Nature is more directed towards the sensible (Nous is not directed towards the sensible at all), but it still has, or is, a knowledge prior to the sensible. Its "weak" products, less real than the true beings in the Nous, reflect its weak type of knowledge.

When production, especially by the Nous, which has clear knowledge, is characterized in the fashion above, a Christian is likely to think of divine knowledge as productive of the world, of creative ideas. We must remember, however, that the Nous is not divine intellect; nor is it the intellect of Plotinus' god, the One. It is simply intellect, simply the Knower.

Further, production by the Nous does not correspond to Christian notions of creation. To name one reason for this, it is not free.[2] Neither the Nous nor nature are free producers. In Plotinus' eyes, to call them free producers would be to denigrate them. They would have to decide whether or not to produce something which "means" nothing to them, something the very knowledge of which would degrade them—something which they cannot seek or choose because if they were capable of search or choice it would not be a fitting object of their search and choice. In a word, free production would be, for Plotinus, an affair of praxis.

Plotinus' teaching that there are instances of knowledge which are immediately productive reflects, therefore, his understanding of the Nous and nature as contemplations, and his view of the relation of the sensible world to these contemplations.

Are there, however, any intimations in human activity of a knowledge which is immediately productive? Plotinus gives the example of geometers who draw figures while contemplating. The point seems to be that they draw figures without what we have called a "special resolve," that the drawing of the figures is a "spontaneous" result of their contemplating. The geometers, however, still bring about a physical result by physical agents, hand and writing instrument.

From our own experience we might add that there seem more generally to be cases in which results in the physical world come about by a spontaneous overflow of knowledge. In the production, for example, of some works of art, while physical means are always employed, the "special resolve" may apparently be absent—further, the aspects of learning, seeking, planning, and correcting may be, if not absent, at least attenuated. It is true that what seems to "overflow" in these cases is not intelligence but the sensuous subconscious. In other cases, where a "special resolve" is combined with a high degree of mastery of materials and technique, learning, planning, and correcting may seem unnecessary—the artist's habitual knowledge can flow directly into the physical effect. But it must be admitted that a higher level of learning, planning, and correcting, taking as its point of departure the artist's habitual knowledge, would be productive of a better artifact.

In cases like that of the engineer, "special resolve" is present, but the engineer does not physically produce the product. His causality is, as we have seen, a causality by thought or knowledge—although his thought must be transmitted by physical means to those who do physically produce the effect. Again the extent to which his skill is perfected is the extent to which his activity becomes less like the planning and replanning of praxis, and more like production by an agent which properly *knows*.

"But," it might be objected, "knowledge may be productive, but can contemplation be productive? Let us grant that for Plotinus contemplation is a kind of knowledge. But is it not speculative knowledge, that is, knowledge that consists only in looking at an object, and is productive of nothing?" The contemplation of which Plotinus speaks is not speculative with regard to sensible things. The Nous and nature do not look at sensible things. They have, or rather are, knowledge—not knowledge of sensible things but knowledge of themselves. This is easily seen in the case of the Nous, which is at once the Knower and the world of true being. What the Nous knows are the true beings within it, not the sensible things in the sensible world. What nature knows, in its diminished fashion, are the vestiges and imitations of true being within it— again not the visible, sensible world.

Plotinus would undoubtedly agree that the sensible world can be contemplated interminably as an object and no results will take place in the sensible world. A "knowledge" consequent upon the sensible world cannot of itself produce results in the sensible world—such a knowledge is determined by the sensible world and does not determine *it*. To effect results in the sensible world based on a viewing of it as object, praxis, which involves physical action, is necessary.

The Nous and nature "contemplate" the sensible world not as an object, but in an act of producing. This is to say that, by a knowledge which is not a viewing of sensible things, but a viewing of what is in themselves, by a knowledge which is prior to sensible things, they produce the sensible universe. Plotinus commonly uses the word "poiesis," or its cognates, to designate the making done by the Nous, the soul, and nature in the manner delineated above. The highest instance of poiesis in his world is, it is true, what can be called the One's autopoiesis; the second highest, the One's production of the Nous. In these cases, however, poiesis is above knowledge, or rather it is an affair of super-knowledge. The

poiesis which concerns us here is the poiesis which, on and below
the level of Nous, Plotinus identifies with contemplation.

Let us examine in further detail the contrast between poiesis
and praxis. The opposition is clearly not, as it is in Aristotle *(Eth.
Nic.* VI, 4–5, 1140a1–b11), one between making and doing, between artistic activity and moral activity. Plotinus' use of the terms
"poiesis" and "praxis" is quite different; the distinction he makes
between them is based on an altogether disparate consideration.
He is talking about results in the sensible world. These results can
be actions or "makings," it makes no difference to him—they are
orderings upon, formings upon, matter. They can come about in
two ways. One is by knowledge, by prior contemplation of the true
realities. A knower which has firm possession by knowledge of the
true beings is automatically productive. Thus the Nous is the
veritable maker of the sensible world. But in this case, the sensible
things fall forth from or come to the producer, without a movement of the producer towards the sensible things. The Nous does
not seek to, plan to, or intend to produce results in the physical
world. The sensible comes to be because the Nous is what it is. The
imitation happens without the imitated exerting any effort to
make it happen. This is poiesis.

We may wonder whether a "making" which takes place on
these terms is making in any recognizable sense. Can there be said
to be making when the maker does not attend at all to the thing
made? Yet Plotinus calls it making, and consistently holds that it is
a type of making superior to ordinary making.

Results in the sensible world can come about also by praxis.
Operating on an inferior level, praxis is, on that level, everything
that poiesis is not. The man of praxis proceeds by deliberation, effort, and physical instruments. He lacks knowledge, in the full
Plotinian sense: he lacks intellectual vision.[3] The urge for praxis is,
however, contemplative in that it is an obscure tentative towards
contemplation. Plotinus tells us that men engage in praxis in order
to have something for themselves, and for others, to see with their
physical eyes (III, 8, 4, 31–39). Seeing is at least analogous to intellectual vision. But is this the reason why things are made? It
would seem not—to many men, at least, this reason would be only
incidental. Things are made for use.

It would appear that in his treatise on contemplation, Plotinus takes a bit of a short-cut. He is aware in other contexts that there are useful arts (cf. IV, 4, 31, 16–19), but instead of mentioning here the way in which use is led back to contemplation, he simply states that even things made by useful art are objects of contemplation—objects of contemplation, that is, for the senses.

He cannot be judged altogether wrong on this point. It is true that very often a maker, a producer, takes pride in seeing the thing made and in showing it to others. The architect, the engineer, the dressmaker like to look at their work, and they like others to look at it. Even "useful" art has a contemplative value. The automobile, the suburban "home"—are they made to use, or to look at? For both purposes, to be sure: but the "speculative" value of these useful things is by no means ignored. Both the makers and the owners wish to look at these things, and desire others to look at them.

What relative values does Plotinus place upon poiesis and upon praxis? Clearly he does not despise, except in a relative sense, the physical world, or what we have called "results in the physical world." The sensible universe is, he says, beautiful, the best possible imitation of the more real world, the world of true being. He does not have what Dewey called a spectator theory of knowledge. The Nous, the veritable Knower, is not a spectator of the physical world, but its producer.

Yet effects in the physical world are inferior which do not flow from a knowledge that is above learning, planning, or seeking. Praxis is inferior to poiesis. This doctrine could be taken simply to mean that the making activity of the Nous is superior to the making activity of men. But we must remember that a man can attain to, can be, the Nous or Knower—by becoming, it is true, more than human, by ceasing to be, properly, a man; nevertheless, a man can become the Knower, can realize his identity with the Knower. This consideration enables Plotinus to devaluate praxis even with regard to men. It is the men whose minds are too weak to contemplate who turn to praxis. It is the duller children who are "directed to works and arts."

Is the man who is able to contemplate, who is able to be the Knower, in a position to take part in poiesis? Can he become the

maker of the world? Plotinus affirms that he can (cf. V, 8, 7, 33–35).
If such an identification with the maker of the world seems illusory, an apologist for Plotinus might point to Plotinus' qualification that man can attain this state only by ceasing to be man, and
further, that once arrived on the level of Nous, he would participate in the most puissant production of the best results in the sensible world—even though they would not be his concern, any
more than they are the concern of the Nous.

It would be unfair to accuse Plotinus of neglecting "making" in
his philosophy: ample provision is made for poiesis; it is highly
regarded. But the net result of his devaluation of praxis in favor of
poiesis would seem, when it is applied to man, to mean a devaluation of real making and doing in favor of illusory making and
doing. The best men would become contemplators, the inferior
men would make and act. For this doctrine Plotinus has been re-
proached with a lack of social, political, and artistic concern.[4]

It seems possible, however, that there is a place in Plotinus'
world for a still recognizably human mode of production which is
above praxis. In the treatise on contemplation, he mentions in
passing a producing which is an accompaniment of contemplation, in the case where "someone" "has something better, prior to
the thing produced, to contemplate" (III, 8, 4, 39–43). In the treatise
"On the Intelligible Beauty," he appears to spell out this notion. He
touches upon the work of the artist, who, he says, does not imitate
nature, but produces according to the ideas, that is, according to
the knowledge-being in the Nous, which nature also imitates. Because of this, he is able to do *better* than nature (V, 8, 1, 32–40).

It is regrettable that Plotinus only touches upon these notions
and does not develop them at greater length.[5] Is the artist's activity
poiesis or praxis? He does not tell us in this passage. It would
appear to fall precisely into neither category. It seems to be a
work overflowing from contemplation. The artist presumably has
"something better, prior to the things produced, to contemplate."
Plotinus mentions that the art in the artist is more perfect than in
the work of art; this would correspond to production by the Nous.
Yet he does use hands and instruments; he probably seeks to
produce and resolves to produce. The notion of the artist's activity

alluded to in this passage would come close to some modern notions of art, even of technology: the necessarily imperfect realization in the physical world, by means of physical effort and instruments, of a "creative idea." Here we do not see the relative folly of praxis. The artist is not a man too weak of intellect to contemplate, who tries to produce something to be seen. He is a genuine intermediary between the Nous and the sensible world, producing results in the sensible world which he seeks, and of which he is conscious, but which reflect his knowledge instead of being remote efforts in the direction of knowledge.

Thus far, in the case of praxis, in the case of poiesis, and in the case of artistic activity, there appears to be genuine making in Plotinus' world. But, after all, are Plotinus' higher makers, the poietic agents such as nature and the Nous, makers in any recognizable sense? It would seem that the maker and the thing made must be separate things. The carpenter, one thing, makes the chair, another thing. Further, the maker expends energy on the thing made. At first glance it appears that the Nous and nature fail to qualify as makers on both of these counts. But let us discuss each of them in more detail.

It is true that the Nous and the sensible world are not, simply speaking, separate things. We have seen in the last chapter that the sensible world, to the extent that it is true being, is the Nous. For the Nous to make the sensible world is not, then, exactly a case of one thing acting upon another. Yet the sensible world is not the world of true being; it is an imitation world, other than and distinct from the Nous to the extent to which it falls short of true being. But can we say that insofar as it is other than the Nous it is caused by the Nous? As it falls short of the Nous, it is a reflection of the Nous upon matter. Does the Nous make matter? Does the Nous make the reflection upon matter?

The closest Plotinus comes to saying that the Nous causes matter is the suggestion, made indirectly in one passage, that the Nous is prior to matter (II, 4, 8, 19–20); and the statement, made elsewhere, that matter is the last of forms (V, 8, 7, 22–23)—all form is either in, or dependent upon, the Nous. It would seem that Plotinus regards matter as a product of the Nous in that it is the end result of the devolution from the Nous. In one place he refers to matter as "a bitter deposit left by the things which precede it" (II, 3, 17, 24).

Is the sensible world truly a product of the Nous? As imitation being, as a reflection upon matter, the sensible world is, if not separate, at least distinct from the Nous. It would seem provisionally to meet the requirement, now modified, that the maker be other than the thing made.

But since the Nous does not expend energy on imitation being, how can it be its *maker*? The imitation being is like a reflection in a mirror. Suppose a man, a visible, physical man, is reflected in a common physical mirror. According to modern notions this happens through transferences of energy. The source of light emits (and so loses) energy, which is mediated by the surface of the man's body (which thus also "loses" the energy) and produces electro-chemical modifications in the mirror. That is, the reflection is caused by energy coming from, though not originating in, the thing reflected. But let us look at the phenomenon in a less sophisticated way. It then seems that, if a mirror is within range of a man, a reflection of the man simply appears in the mirror. There is nothing apparent leaving the man to go to the mirror. He seems to lose nothing, yet he *causes* his reflection. The reflection is "real" because of the man. No man—no reflection of a man. No thing whatever—no reflection at all. But the man is not expending himself, or his "creativity," or his ideas, to produce the reflection.

For Plotinus, the case a step higher is parallel to this. The true beings do not expend themselves, their "creativity," their knowledge, upon the sensible things which are their reflections. But the sensible things are real because of the true beings. If there were no true beings there would be no sensible things.

If, still pursuing the mirror analogy, we ask whether the true beings make the sensible things, we see that it is like asking if the man makes his reflection in a mirror. Perhaps if we were asked what makes a reflection, say a reflection of a horse, in a mirror, we would not say "the horse," but would again enter into some scientific explanation of reflection. Yet we speak, in a less sophisticated fashion, of a hand, for example, making a shadow on a wall.[6] And if instead of asking someone "What makes the reflection of a horse in a mirror?" we were to point to an actual reflection and say "What is making that reflection?" the answer might well be "A horse."

Let us suppose, then, that the thing reflected makes the reflection in a mirror. Even if we are willing to grant that this is a case of actual making, what is our reaction when Plotinus tells us that this typifies a more potent making than does the activity of the sculptor in making the statue?

When a shadow is cast or a reflection made in a mirror, the making seems too effortless, the product too ephemeral. Here appears the notion that true making requires effort. There is, in fact, a tendency to equate the efficiency of making with effort: the greater the effort, the more truly effective is the making. It can be shown, however, that such an equation does not hold. As we have seen above, the engineer, the architect, etc., are recognized as makers, but they do not exert physical effort. It might popularly be thought that the better engineer is simply the one who uses the most "mental" effort, but probably it would be seen after explanation that intelligence, training, and experience might enable one engineer, employing less effort, to be better as an engineer than another who uses more effort. As regards physical effort, it is quite generally understood that the craftsman with a superior technique produces better works with less effort.

Nonetheless, what can be powerful about a making upon which *no* effort is expended? In the case of the image in the mirror, at least, the material, if it can be called a material, is perfectly pliable. It is non-resistant to the imposition of the form. It makes no demands for itself. The image is the best possible image. The proof of this is that it can be mistaken for the original more easily than any other image. Further, the reflection in a mirror is not a reality on the same level with the reflected. The reflection is more fully controlled by, and more properly inferior to (ontically beneath), the reflected, than is a statue, for example, with reference to the sculptor. It is more properly dependent; if we dare say it, it is more *caused*.

Plotinus does not suppose that reflections and shadows are the superior products of the makers operating in the sensible world. He would say, as we do, that the man who produces a statue or a bridge produces something more real than a shadow or a reflection. His argument is, rather, that the latter type of production resembles, more closely than the former, the production of the sensible universe by the Nous. Why? Not because he wishes to detract from the reality of the product, but because he insists on the greater reality of the producer. Sensible realities, changeable, spatially deployed, are altogether less than the Nous. Unless he is to represent the Nous after the model of the sensible universe, he cannot present the causing of the sensible things by the Nous as a causing of something which is relatively on the same level as its cause. The Nous does not cause something as solid, as substantial, as real, as itself. This would be to make another Nous, or at least another "true being." But, as we have seen in the last chapter, the sensible universe truly is, in relation to the Nous, ephemeral and insubstantial, just as the mirror-image is, in relation to a sensible thing, ephemeral and insubstantial. So for Plotinus the making of a reflection in a mirror appears to be the most suitable analogy to the making of sensible realities by the Nous. The maker (the Nous) and the things made (the sensible things) are both real, and the Nous really makes the sensible things. But because the Nous is more real than the sensible things it makes, the making is analogous to the making of an image in a mirror.

Can this real making be considered a case of "efficient causality?" The Aristotelian cause, which has come to be called the efficient cause, is described by Aristotle himself as ". . . that from which is the first beginning of change or of rest, as the advisor is a cause, and the father a cause of the son, and universally the maker of the thing made, and the changer of the thing changed."[7] The examples which Aristotle gives, in several places, are, as above, the advisor and the father, and also, the building art and the medical art, the seed, and the soul as cause of the body.[8]

Now, for Aristotle, movement is in the thing moved. The actuality of making is in the thing made; the actuality of house-building is in the house which is built. Whenever something else comes to be from something, the ultimate actuality is in the product. Aristotle contrasts this situation with those activities in which there is no product beyond the "work" itself, activities such as seeing and contemplating. Here the act is in the one who sees, in the contemplator, not in anything else (*Metaph.* Theta, 8, 1050a23–b2).

These views fit in with Aristotle's notion of contemplation as being, in itself, divorced from poiesis and praxis. While, as we have seen, these words have a different meaning for Aristotle than they have for Plotinus, together they still cover "the production of results in the sensible world."

The actuality of efficient causality is, then, for Aristotle, in the product. Co-ordinately, a contemplator *qua* contemplator cannot be an efficient cause. For Plotinus, on the contrary, a contemplator is a maker. The Nous, soul, and nature make and generate things. When he says this he quite possibly has Aristotle's separation of making from contemplating specifically in mind.[9]

The Nous, a contemplative producer, makes the sensible world. Is the actuality of the making in the Nous, or in the sensible world? Plotinus, so far as I can see, does not tell us in so many words where the actuality *of the making* is. The Nous is surely self-contained; its own actuality is entirely within it; in fact, its own actuality is its very being. But it makes, it produces, precisely because it is in itself and towards itself. Plotinus might call the thing made (either the soul or the sensible world) the act *from* the Nous, according to his distinction between act *of* and act *from*. (*Vide supra*, p. 28.) His concern is with the absolute superiority, the "more reality" of the Nous as a producer, with its complete self-possession, with the entire dependence of its product upon *it*.

These things granted, he might even agree with Aristotle that the making is in the thing made, much as for St. Thomas Aquinas creation is real in the created but not in the creator.[10] Regarding the One, Plotinus says "To call it a cause is not to attribute anything accidental to it, but to ourselves; for we have something from it, while it is in itself." (VI, 9, 3, 49–51; cf. VI, 8, 7, 44–46.)

The fact remains that the higher makers, the Nous and of course the One, are for Plotinus more than, and therefore different from, the causes envisaged by Aristotle when he described what has come to be called efficient cause. It is significant that Aristotle almost never refers to his highest causes, the Separate Entities, as makers; he did not, apparently, consider them efficient causes.[11] For Plotinus, on the other hand, the highest causes are called consistently makers and generators. It would be strange indeed if this were a mere matter of differing terminologies. Plotinus seems to mean that the Nous makes the soul and the sensible world, not in the same way a builder makes a house, but in a way analogous to this. For Aristotle, the Separate Entities are final causes, that is, objects of desire (*Metaph.* Lambda, 7, 1072a19–b13). The Nous is an object of desire, but when Plotinus speaks of its causing, he does not speak of its *causing as an object of desire*. It causes by *making* imitations. The conclusion must be that Plotinus has in mind something we must call real efficient causality. It is not, to be sure, the efficient causality envisaged by Aristotle. Yet as the Nous is a maker, so it is an efficient cause. Plotinus has seen an extension of "making" into regions where Aristotle did not suppose that it existed. And if we are at all able to appreciate Plotinus' argument that the Nous is more real than the sensible world, we will also understand that the Nous is more properly an efficient cause than are efficient causes in the sensible world, that it is, as he says, the ontic maker, the *poiêtês ontôs*.

To what extent can these characterizations of the Nous as efficient cause be applied to nature? Generally speaking, it is just a matter of watering down what has been said about Nous. Nature is a "better" efficient cause than is a sensible maker, and it is "worse" than Nous. Like the Nous, nature is that for which Aristotle makes no provision, a contemplative maker; but it has an obscure contemplation, a less perfect poiesis, and—if soul rather than the visible cosmos be taken to be the primary product of the Nous—a weaker product.

The common notion of making, as we have seen, allows not only for the action of a physical agent upon a physical thing, but also for a "thinker" or a "planner" as an agent. Plotinus' "praxis" corresponds almost entirely with making understood in this broader sense. It is real making.

Poiesis, the making done by the more real producers, the Nous, the soul, and nature, is not merely connected with knowledge, with contemplation, but is identical with them. In the doctrine of poiesis, Plotinus has extended significantly the notion of making: poiesis is more real making.

Poiesis, as Plotinus sees it, does not correspond exactly to Aristotle's efficient causality. But as a genuine making, which seems analogous to ordinary making and is not coincident with either formal or final causality, it can be called a real efficient causality.

NOTES

1. Cf. VI, 4, 10, 5 –11; V, 8, 1; III, 8, 2, 6 –12; IV, 4, 31, 16 –17.

2. This is at least a *prima facie* opposition. If both Plotinus' position and that of a Christian theology heavily influenced by Greek conceptions are investigated in depth, it is possible to display the two views as fairly close to one another.

3. The distinction which Plotinus makes between poiesis and praxis is apparently unique. As Arnou observes, "Ainsi donc, en laissant de côté ceux pour qui la distinction n'existe pas, soit chez Platon, soit chez Aristote, soit chez les commentateurs autorisés du Stagirite qu'on lisait à l'école de Plotin, quand on opposait *poiein* et *prattein*, *prattein* désignait toujours, avec des nuances qui varient de Platon à Aristote, une mode d'action moralement supérieure. . . . La conception d'une *praxis* engagée dans le sensible, en contraste avec une *poièsis* libre, pure, élevée, qui est la contemplation même, cette conception, ou plutôt ce vocabulaire (on a vu que c'était celui de Plotin), n'est pas en usage chez ses précurseurs." (René Arnou, *praxis et theôria*, Paris, 1921, pp. 36 –37.) It must not be supposed, however, that Plotinus' use of these terms is perfectly consistent. *Vide* Appendix I, translation of III, 8, 2 and III, 8, 4.

4. Cf. e.g., Joseph Katz, *Plotinus' Search for the Good* (New York, 1950), pp. 30–34. There is, to be sure, the story given by Porphyry, ch. 12, that Plotinus asked the emperor Gallienus to restore a ruined city in Campania and give it to the philosophers, to be ruled by Plato's laws and known as Platonopolis. Henry remarks that this "would have been a monastery of contemplatives."

5. The reason may be that the doctrine of V, 8, valuable though it be, is not Plotinus' usual view of art. In IV, 3, 10, 17–19, we read: "Art is posterior to nature and imitates it by making weak and beclouded imitations, toys of little worth, while using many mechanical devices to imitate nature." Both V, 8, (chronological number 31) and IV, 3 (chronological number 27) are treatises from Group II, and therefore both were written within the same six-year period.

6. The sensible world is a "shadow," just as it is a "reflection," of the Nous. Cf. III, 8, 11, 25 –29.

7. *Metaph.* Delta, 2, 1013a29 –32. Substantially the same description is given in *Phys.* II, 3, 194b29 –32.

8. *Metaph.* Lambda, 4, 1070b26; *Phys.* II, 3, 195a22; *De An.*, II, 4, 415b10.

9. Commentators have noted that the first chapter of the treatise on contemplation, III, 8, 1, contains echoes of Aristotle's treatment of contemplation in Book X of the *Nichomachean Ethics*. *(Vide,* e.g., Bréhier's *Notice* to III, 8 in the latter's edition of the *Enneads*, III, 149.) Plotinus therefore seems to have Aristotle's doctrine specifically in mind when he begins to treat of contemplation. It is patent that he alters this doctrine drastically, not only by extending contemplation to brute animals and to plants, but also, and more important, by making contemplation productive. According to Aristotle's explicit statement, in this very book, contemplation is not productive—in fact, it is opposed to production. *(Eth. Nic.* X, 8, 1178b20–21.)

10. ". . . creatio in creatura non sit nisi relatio quaedam ad creatorem, ut ad principium sui esse." "Relatio in Deo ad creaturam non est realis. . . ; Relatio vero creaturae ad Deum est relatio realis. . . ." *(Summa Th.* I, 45, 3c. et ad 1.)

11. Cf. Joseph Owens, *The Doctrine of Being in the Aristotelian Metaphysics* (Toronto, 1963), p. 467. For a discussion of interpretations of Aristotle which take the Separate Entities as efficient causes, cf. *ibid.*, p. 468, n. 45.

10

WHAT FINAL meaning does the doctrine of nature as contemplation have in Plotinus' philosophy? If there is truly a downward gradation of being, thought, and poietic strength from Nous to the higher part of the World Soul to nature, the teaching of *Ennead* III, 8, satisfactorily represents his position. The visible cosmos is nature's product of contemplation. If, on the other hand, there is a direct presence of the Nous to matter, so that matter is "formed" immediately by its contact with true being, the visible cosmos is, it would seem, a direct product of the Nous, and intermediation by soul and nature, the "logizing" of matter through these bearers of intellectuality, is unnecessary. The whole doctrine of soul and nature would be beside the point, and, if not opposed to the doctrine of the omnipresence of being, then only a metaphorical expression of it.

Plotinus is not at all embarrassed by the opposition suggested here. His presentation of the omnipresence of being, centered in *Ennead* VI, 4 and 5, begins by raising the question of *soul's presence to extended body,* and once the question of the presence of the intelligible universe (the Nous, true being) to the visible cosmos is raised, he moves easily from the one theme to the other. This indicates that in his mind the two perspectives were not disparate. In presenting the visible universe as the direct participation of Nous, he has not abandoned the notion of the part played by soul. He does not, however, either in these treatises or elsewhere, furnish an obvious articulation of the two positions.

The investigations of the philosophic import of Plotinus' doctrine in chapters 8 and 9 have enabled us to see this technical problem in a fresh light. The sensible world, we discover, is as real for him as for anyone; the nature, the "beingness," of the sensible world is also real. In holding that nature is a contemplation, he is not holding that it is something ephemeral, but rather that it is something more real, more "solid" than the material world. The world of true being, the Nous, is, in turn, still more real: more real than both nature and the sensible world. It too is a contemplation.

We see that when Plotinus speaks of production he is fully cognizant of the ordinary producing done by artisans, and that this ordinary producing is fully real for him. When he speaks of contemplative producers, the Nous and nature, he understands them to be the more real producers, more powerfully productive. Both of them are genuine efficient causes of the real sensible world. If for Plotinus the sensible world has these two real producers, then we must ask how he can speak as though it proceeded directly from only the Nous, the higher of the two.

As we have seen, Plotinus has only one world. That world, its being, its entity, consists in the true beings, which are identical with the Nous, the veritable Knower. Only the Knower, of course, can know the world as it truly is. This means, if we may employ the spatial metaphor, that Plotinus' world of true being is right here. It is not a heaven of ideas. Taken in this way, the world is not caused by the Nous, except insofar as, within the Nous, intellect is sometimes said to cause the intelligibles. It *is* the Nous.

The world of true being has an imitation: the world which presents itself to sense and opinion. The imitation is not unreal, but is decisively less real than the true being. The only being in the imitation is true being and only to the extent that it is there. But more properly, the imitation is in the true being; the world of true being contains its own imitation. The imitation is produced by the true being in a way similar to that in which an image in a mirror is produced by the thing reflected. Therefore the Nous could be called the formal cause of the being in the imitation—if there were any being in the imitation—and the efficient cause of the imitation as an imitation.

The function of intermediaries in this production may be looked at both negatively and positively. Negatively, the presence of intermediaries will not interfere with the Nous. If there are less-reals intervening in some fashion between the Nous and the sensible, imitation world, the intermediation can be only as real as the intermediaries. The presence of intermediaries—the higher soul and nature—cannot prevent the Nous from being the only veritable entity which the world has. Nor can it prevent the Nous from being the only true-being cause of any of its imitations—the higher soul, nature, or the ultimate imitation, the sensible universe. The only contemplative producer of the world which has "true" contemplation, that is, an identification of knowledge with veritable being, is the Nous. Therefore, even if there are intermediaries between the Nous and its imitation, the imitation will still be caused by contemplative producing by the Nous.

The causality of the Nous cannot be transmitted to soul, and through soul to nature and the sensible cosmos, as though it were a physical causality transmitted through a chain of causes, all of which were on the same level of reality. The Nous, soul, and nature are not on the same level of reality. The mode of the transmission of the Nous's causality can be illustrated by expanding Plotinus' mirror analogy. Consider a horse reflected in a mirror, and the reflection in turn reflected in another, and that in another . . . the "what" will always be the same; the reflection, so long as it preserves any distinctness at all, will be "a horse," and it will be made by nothing else, at the level of true being, as opposed to imitation being, than a horse.

Similarly, the sensible world, by imitating nature, imitates nothing but the Nous on the level of being. If it is made by the contemplative activity of nature on nature's own level, it is still made by nothing but the Nous on the level of being.

Plotinus himself, in what is called the treatise "On Intelligible Beauty," can say, "It remains, therefore, that all things are in another; and with nothing in between, by the proximity in being towards another, there appears suddenly a likeness and image of the intelligible world, *whether from it directly (autothen), or by the ministration of soul*—this makes no difference in the present argument—or of a particular soul." (V, 8, 7, 13–16.) Here again

Plotinus affirms the doctrine of *Ennead* III, 6, and VI, 4 and 5. By making use of the corrections of metaphor offered in those treatises, it is easy to interpret the expressions used here. The sensible world, the image of the intelligible, does not appear, strictly speaking, because of the "proximity" of the intelligible world, nor even because of its "presence," unless these words are emptied of all spatial connotation. Nor does it appear "suddenly," unless this word be taken in an a-temporal sense. The intelligible world is being, a-extended and a-temporal. The sensible world has imitation order and form through its striving for the intelligible world, the mere existence of which renders this striving actual.

The sensible world appears by the "proximity" of the intelligible, *whether there is a ministration by soul or not.* It is now safe to say that Plotinus means here, "even though there is, in fact, a ministration by soul."

Nature, the lower part of the Soul of the All, is the being of the visible cosmos insofar as it is the bearer of logos, that is, insofar as it is, however remotely, Nous. Thus Plotinus is able to pay little regard to the question whether the appearance of the visible cosmos about the Nous is *autothen* from the Nous or not. To the extent that the ministering hypostasis or hypostases are being, to the extent that they have a share in the contemplative producing of the visible cosmos, they are Nous. Thus the Nous, to the extent that it produces through a medium, produces through a transparent medium. The "producing" is *autothen* whether there is a medium or not.

Therefore, to say that the sensible world is the direct product of Nous and to say that it is the product of Nature's contemplation are to say the same thing, because to the extent that Nature's contemplation is intellectual and thus productive, it is Nous.

Positively, it can be shown that, granted the outlines of Plotinus' view of the world, there must be intermediaries between the Nous and the sensible world. And yet it must be admitted that, as our insight into the nature of soul progressively deepens, there seems to be a danger that soul, in the real order, will be seen to be absorbed into Nous on the one hand and into the sensible world on the other.

We are first told that soul, the highest part of which is rooted in the intelligible world, descends to the sensible as the bearer of logos. This descending to the sensible is the producing of the sensible. The more soul descends, the less real, the less contemplative, the less productive it becomes. Nature, the lowest part of soul, the least productively contemplative, produces the lowest reality, the sensible cosmos.

And yet how can soul, insofar as it is rooted in the world of true being, actually descend? It cannot: Plotinus says in one place that it "appears to descend." The "descent" of soul is a metaphor; it can be balanced by another metaphor: the lower reaches for the higher, matter attempts to seize being and intelligibility. Perhaps nature as contemplation is rather the result of an effort from below. It is, perhaps, the imitation being and intelligibility which matter has seized for itself.

Yet the notion of matter "trying to seize" being is metaphorical. Matter has no power. What appears to be present in matter is present because of the productive power of the Nous. Therefore, if in truth there is no descent, and if there is no effort from below, perhaps soul is merely Nous considered as related (although Nous actually is not related) to the visible cosmos. A similar explanation might be applied to the lower "parts" of soul. In this case nature would be Nous considered as related to plants, the earth, and the vegetative functions in animals.

If the higher part of soul is in the intelligible world, is it in any way distinct from Nous? Is not "soul" an unnecessary term for something which is really Nous? And what of the "lower part"? If it is not Nous, it would seem to be purely sensible, purely imitation, cut off from Nous and being, indistinguishable therefore from the sensible world. And thus soul would disappear as an hypostasis. Soul and nature would be only logically distinct from Nous, and there would be, in the real order, only the Nous and the sensible world.

Plotinus, however, neither says this nor means this. For him, soul is an hypostasis, a nature, a reality, really distinct from Nous; thus nature, as the lower part of soul, would be distinct from Nous as a distinct hypostasis—or part of a distinct hypostasis. The world contains whatever is, to any degree, real. Further, there is for

Plotinus a rigorous correspondence between thought and thing. If the world can be known in a certain way, that is because it is in a certain way. If it is in a certain way, it can be known in that way.

Thus there is not only sense and intellect; not only the imitation world and the world of true being. The world can be known as Nous, as true being. But it can be known also as Nous with a mission to form and order matter, therefore no longer perfectly as Nous, but as soul—and this is to know something real. And again, the world can be known as soul no longer capable of producing within itself, but capable only of producing upon matter—this again is to know something real, nature.

In short, the world can be viewed truly as Nous. It can be viewed relatively truly as soul, as nature, as sensible. All of these aspects, which Plotinus *sees*, are in the world.

The Nous and the intermediaries are more than logically distinct. In all the ways the world can be thought, so it is. It can be known as Nous—it is Nous. It can be known, by a diminished knowledge, as soul—it is soul. It can be known as nature—it is nature. The Nous is a distinct hypostasis to the extent that it is not the One. Soul is a distinct hypostasis to the extent that it is not Nous, not contemplation, not being. Nature is a distinct hypostasis, or part of a distinct hypostasis, in the same way.

As the Nous is the being of the sensible universe *via* soul, the One is the super-being of Nous. The Nous "makes" the sensible universe, it is the veritable maker, in the sense that the sensible universe appears, happens, because the Nous, which is being, *is*. In a similar fashion the Nous happens because the One supersubsists. Plotinus' treatment of the generation of the Nous by the One and his treatment of the production of the sensible world by the Nous are parallel. The primordial sensible world is matter which "tries to seize being" and so becomes an imitation of being. Similarly, the primordial Nous is presented as an intellectual-intelligible matter which "turns to the One" in an attempt to receive oneness and so stabilizes itself as intellect and intelligibility (cf. V, 2, 1, 7–13; VI, 7, 16, 10–35). It goes without saying that in both cases there is no temporal sequence involved. But stripped of metaphor, these notions mean that the otherness, the non-oneness, of the Nous, its intelligible matter, is the gauge of its separation from the One. But for this, it would be the One, just as, if it were not for matter, the sensible universe would be the Nous. The Nous, as one, is the One, just as the sensible world, as being, is the Nous—but the Nous, as a second one, is not the One, and the sensible world, as an imitation of the Nous, is not the Nous.

These considerations permit a final evaluation of Plotinus' notion of poiesis. An inferior hypostasis is generated without any outflowing motion of the hypostasis of the generator. Absolutely nothing leaves the One to come to the Nous, and nothing leaves the Nous to come to the soul or to the sensible cosmos. There is, further, no exertion in causal efficacy. That which is generated comes to hypostasis eternally, or rather a-temporally, in relation to the generator. And yet the generated cannot be regarded as a distinct existent, because its being, or in the case of the Nous, its super-being, is the generator.

When speaking of the production of the sensible world by soul, Plotinus strives to hold this notion of production, and yet to permit some declination towards matter. In doing so, he toys with the notion of multiplying hypostases, or parts of hypostases, between the higher soul and matter. But ultimately the declination towards matter is seen to be metaphor. The relaxation of unity, contemplation, and poietic strength in the descent from the Nous is not so much an actual relaxing, as the presence, on different levels, of realities which, although still real, and still mirror images of true being, are progressively less and less real. Since Plotinus sees these inferior realities, soul and nature, present "between" the Nous and the sensible cosmos, a presentation of these intermediaries is necessary to make his view of his world complete.

It has become clear that the formulation of Plotinus' philosophy benefits from the doctrine of contemplative producing provided in *Ennead* III, 8. If we did not possess *Ennead* III, 8, it would be possible to reconstruct its doctrines, in essence, from indications elsewhere in the *Enneads*. What would be lacking, however, and what *Ennead* III, 8 provides, is precisely contemplative producing as a synthesizing principle. Contemplative producing, interpreted to be sure in the light of other doctrines and other synthetic notions, is seen to co-ordinate best Plotinus' picture of his world. With regard to nature, it is the notion which connects nature most suitably through soul with Nous: this is of decisive importance, because Nous is the true being of the world. It also unifies the other notions, such as life and logos, which are appropriate to a Plotinian description of nature. In this sense "contemplative producer" is the ultimate characterization of the nature in vegetative things for the world of Plotinus, and Plotinus' philosophy needs the doctrine of nature as contemplation.

A TRANSLATION OF ENNEAD III, 8, 1–4

III, 8, 1 Playing at first, before we handle our subject seriously, if we were to say that all things desire contemplation and look to this end, not only rational but also irrational animals, and the nature in plants and the earth which engenders them, and that all gain it, each one having it according to the nature of each, but that different ones gain contemplation in different ways, some truly, while others get an imitation and image thereof—would anyone sustain so paradoxical a statement?

But since this has come up among ourselves there will arise no danger in our playing in our own affairs. But, now, do we not, in our present play, contemplate? Indeed we and all who play do (*poiousin*) this, or rather they play because they desire contemplation. And, at a venture, whether some boy or some man plays or is in earnest, it is for the sake of contemplation that he plays, and that he is in earnest; and all practical activity (*praxis*) has its urge towards contemplation—the necessary, which draws contemplation more fully to the external, or what is called voluntary, which draws it less; nevertheless it itself is done through a desire for contemplation.

But of all that later. Now let us say of the earth itself and of trees and of all plants, what is their contemplation; and how those things made and generated from it [the earth] are led back to the activity of contemplation; and how nature, which they say is without imagination and without reason, has a contemplation in itself, and produces what it produces by the contemplation which it "does not have"; and how . . .

III, 8, 2

Now that nature has, then, neither hands nor feet nor any instrument, adventitious or natural, but that it needs matter, upon which it will produce (*poiêsei*), and which it makes in form[1]—this is evident to everyone. It is necessary also to remove levering from nature's producing (*poiêseôs*). For what thrust or what lever makes the many-colored and manifold patterns? Since the molders in wax or the image-makers, whom beholders indeed have supposed to be very like the working of nature, cannot make colors but take from elsewhere the colors which they use. But we must realize that, for the pursuit of such arts, it is necessary that there be something remaining stable in them [the artisans], according to which stable thing they make (*poiêsousin*), by [the use of] hands, their works, and similarly there must be something of this sort in nature, which must be stable and thus is a power, which produces (*poiousan*), not by hands, and is altogether stable.

For it is not necessary that there be [parts] as it were stable, other [parts] as it were moving—matter is the moved, [but] there is nothing of nature[2] which is moved—rather that will not be the first movent—nature will not be that, but the unmoved in the All. But logos, someone may say, is unmoved, but nature is other than logos and is moved. But if they speak of the whole [of nature] logos too [would move]. And if something of it is unmoved, this is logos.

For, also, nature must be a form (*eidos*), and not composed of matter and form. For what need does it have of matter hot or cold? The underlying matter which it works over comes to it possessed of these qualities, or rather, not having these qualities [of itself], it receives them by being logized (*logôtheisa*). For, in order that matter may become fire, it is not necessary that fire come, but rather the logos [of fire]. Which is a not insignificant indication that there are productive (*poiountas*) logoi in animals and in plants, and that nature is a logos which produces (*poiei*) another logos akin to it, which other logos gives something to the substratum while itself remaining immobile. The logos according to the visible form (*morphê*) is the last logos, dead, and unable at all to produce another, while the logos which has life is brother to that which produces the form (*morphê*), and, having the same power as the latter, produces [the form] in the thing which is engendered (*poiei en tô(i) genomenô(i)*).

[The latter part of this passage, with its mention of various logoi, is susceptible of two plausible interpretations:

1) Plotinus might be referring to an ordering of logoi down from nature. In this case, he would seem to establish four logoi: (*a*) Nature. (*b*) The immovable, which gives something to the substrate (produces the form). (*c*) The living, which produces (acts) in the constituted being. (*d*) The inert, which is referred to the visible form. This interpretation would establish the passage as an answer to a question proposed in a possibly earlier treatise, "The form which nature gives to the thing which it fashions must be considered different from nature itself; but we must enquire whether there is still an intermediary between this form and nature." (IV, 4, (28), 14, 8–11.) If our interpretation of the ordering of the logoi is correct, Plotinus has introduced (*b*) as the intermediary between nature and the form it gives the thing which it fashions, and has distinguished in the latter form the living (*c*) and the inert (*d*). He would thus seem to have in mind the producing of the whole visible cosmos by nature, through the intermediation of logoi.

2) Alternatively, Plotinus may be talking about the production of one animal or plant by another as an imparting of logos. In this case the passage would mean that the nature, the immoblile living logos of the generator, would produce the living logos of the generated, a logos akin to it and having the same power it has. The living logos (nature) of the generator would produce the visible form of the generator, while the living logos (nature) of the generated would produce the visible form of the generated. To interpret the passage in this way we must supply *morphên* as the object of *poiei* in the last line.

To read this passage in the light of III, 8, 4, where the product of nature's contemplating-producing is designated by this same word, *to genomenon,* yet seems plainly to mean the visible ("a product of contemplation splendid and graceful," *ibid.*, lines 21–22), is to lend support to the first interpretation. But this interpretation involves the somewhat forced rendering of the *poiei* in the last line as "acts." Further, the mention of matter becoming fire by the coming of the logos of fire suggests a temporal becoming which would be parallel to the temporal generation of an individual animal, rather than to the a-temporal generation of the whole visible cosmos by nature. For these reasons the second interpretation is the probable here.]

III, 8, 3

In what way does it produce? How, producing in this way, might it attain a certain contemplation? Rather, if it produces in remaining stable and remaining in itself, and is a logos, it may be itself a contemplation. For praxis, which would come to be according to logos, is obviously other than logos: logos, which accompanies praxis and governs it, would not be praxis. If, now, it [nature] is not praxis but logos, it is contemplation. And in the whole range of logos, the *last* is from contemplation and is contemplation in the sense that it is contemplated (*tetheôrêmenos*); while in all logos which is before this there is the logos which is different in different things, which is not nature but soul, and there is the logos which is in nature and is nature.

Is it itself [the logos which is nature] [derived] from contemplation? It is entirely from contemplation. But if it had been contemplative of itself? But how? For it is the end product of a contemplation and of a certain contemplator.

How does it itself have contemplation? It does not have contemplation from reasoning (*ek logou*): I call "contemplation from reasoning" a searching about the things which are in it. Why not, when it is a certain life and a logos and a productive power? Is it that to search is to not yet have? Nature possesses, and for this reason, namely that it possesses, it produces. For nature, to be what it is is its poiesis (*to poiein*), and as it is, so is its making. But it is contemplation and theorema, for it is a logos. Now by being contemplation and theorema and logos—by being these, nature produces.

Thus poiesis is revealed to us to be contemplation: it is the end product of a contemplation which remains contemplation, not making (*praxasês*) anything else, but producing (*poiêsasês*) by being contemplation.

III, 8, 4

And if anyone asks nature for what end she produces (*poiei*), if she consents to hear the questioner and to speak, she will say: "You must not question me; you must understand, and yourself be silent, just as I am silent and am not accustomed to speak. What, then, must you understand? That the thing produced is my product of contemplation (*theama*), silence [sic], and my natural theorema, and I too am born from a similar contemplation, and have the nature of a lover of contemplation. And my contemplating makes a theorema, as geometers draw while contemplating: but when I, drawing nothing, contemplate, the lines of bodies come to be, falling forth, as it were [from me]. And I have the disposition of my mother and of the beings which generated me: for these too are [derived] from contemplation, and my generation while they themselves made (*praxantôn*) nothing—but as they are better logoi, in contemplating themselves I am generated."

What do these words wish to say? That what is called nature is a soul, the offspring of a prior soul which lives more powerfully, having in its quiet self a contemplation [directed] not towards the above, nor again towards the below; standing in what it is, in its own stasis and in a sort of synesthesis, by this synesis and synesthesis it sees what is after it, in such a way as is fitting to it, and it does not seek further, but accomplishes its theorema, splendid and graceful.

And if anyone wishes to accord to nature a certain synesis or perception, it is not as we speak of perception or synesis in others, but as if one were to compare the [synesis and perception] of sleep (or dream, *tou hypnou*) to those of one who is awake.

For in contemplating the theorema born to it, nature rests, because it remains in itself and with itself and is [itself] a theorema. And it is a silent, weaker contemplating. There is another contemplation more active for viewing; this is an image of that other contemplation. In this way, what is born from it is altogether weak, because a weakening contemplation makes a weak product of con-templation: because men also, when they are weak in the direction of contemplating, make praxis (*praxin poiountai*), [praxis which is] a shadow of contemplation and logos. For when the [power] of contemplation is not suitable to them because of weakness of soul, not being able to understand the object of contemplation (*theama*) suitably, and therefore not being full, but attempting to see it, they are borne to praxis, so that they may see what they cannot see by intellect. When indeed they make [something] (*poiôsi*), they wish that both they themselves may see it and others may see and per-ceive it, when their purpose is, as much as this is possible, praxis.[3]

For in all cases we shall find that poiesis and praxis are either a weakening of, or an accompaniment of, contemplation: a weaken-ing, if someone does not have anything beyond the thing made (*prachthen*); an accompaniment, if he has something better, prior to the thing produced (*poiêthentos*), to contemplate. For why would the man who is able to contemplate the true go by preference to the image of the true? And the duller children bear witness, who, ill-disposed to the possibility of learning and contemplation, are reduced to arts and works.

NOTES

1. Ficino: "ponat in specie."

2. Perhaps "of that power."

3. Inge, I, 160: "when their object is, as far as possible, expressed in action."

APPENDIX II

"NATURE" AND "CONTEMPLATION" IN THE GREEK TRADITION

PHYSIS "Physis," the Greek word commonly translated "nature," is derived from the root *phy-* by the addition of the nominal suffix *-sis*. "Physis" is connected with *phyein* "make to grow," *phyesthai* "grow," *ho phus* "offspring," and *to phyton* "plant." In view of these affinities, "physis" might be taken to mean radically, "growing," "growth," or "principle of growth." The root *phy-*, however, which is cognate with the Sanskrit *bhū-* "be, become," the Latin *fui* and *fieri*, and the English "be," seems able to bear the more basic meaning "be." "Physis," accordingly, can mean "being," or, with a somewhat abstractive force, "beingness"—"the intrinsic constitution of a thing," its "nature" in this still quite familiar sense.

When "physis" occurs in the pre-Socratic fragments it often appears to have this meaning. Cf. Heraclitus fr. 1, fr. 106; Parmenides fr. 16; Empedocles fr. 63; possibly Parmenides fr. 10 and Empedocles fr. 8. In some instances "physis," while retaining the basic meaning of intrinsic constitution, beingness, seems also to carry the notion of matter, stuff. This is not strange since the pre-Socratics knew only, and were dealing only with, material being. On occasion it seems to mean birth or generation (as perhaps in the latter two fragments).[1]

Plato frequently uses "physis" in the sense of beingness or intrinsic constitution. Cf. e.g., Rep. 525c; *Philebus*, 44e; *Politicus*, 269d; *Sophist*, 265a; *Parmenides*, 132d.

Aristotle, in *Metaph.* Delta, 4, 1014b16–1015a19, surveys five meanings of "physis," meanings connected with coming to be, growth, principle of growth, and ousia (beingness, entity), and offers his own definition, which contains elements of all the preceding meanings, in the form of a conclusion: "From what has been said, physis first and properly so called is the ousia of those things which have in themselves, as themselves, a source of movement." Aristotle was not interested in startling etymological tricks, or in definitions which would altogether subvert common meanings. Both the five listed meanings and the synthetic meaning arrived at in the end must have had a firm basis in Greek usage up to his time.

It seems plausible to combine the above definition with two definitions of "physis" in the *Physics*: ". . . physis is a certain source and cause of being moved and being at rest in that to which it belongs first, according to itself and not accidentally . . ." (*Phys.* II, 1, 192b21–23); and: ". . . physis could be the *morphê* and *eidos* of those things which have in themselves a source of motion . . ." (*ibid.*, 193b4–5). Thus Aristotle's meaning is that physis is the ousia, that is, the form, that is, the intrinsic source of movement, of such things as have an intrinsic source of movement. Ousia, form, and source of movement are in the case of these things identical.

Aristotle's definition welds together the "being" and "growth" meanings of "physis." While the etymologically first meaning may be equivalent to "ousia" itself, the philosophic outlook of the pre-Socratics had already restricted "physis" to material things. "Physis" also had meanings associated with those of *phyesthai*, as "grow," and, by extension "become." Aristotle's contribution, philosophic rather than etymological, was the realization that the ousia of a changeable, material thing is its intrinsic principle of "growth," or movement.

After Aristotle, "physis" would primarily connote the beingness, the reality of material things, especially of those which grow and reproduce, but by extension, of all those which change, with a disposition to treat that beingness as a source of growth and change. This, presumably, would be the meaning, or complex of meanings, which "physis" would evoke originally for Plotinus and his hearers.

The "collective" sense of nature is, however, occasionally in evidence, as in Aristotle's doctrine of the unmoved movent: "From such a principle, then, depend the heavens and (the world of) nature" (*Metaph.* Lambda, 7, 1072b13–14). Also, "physis" can have the more general meaning of the "beingness," the "nature" of anything, as when in *Metaph.* Gamma, 2, 1003a33–b6 he speaks of "the nature of being."

THEORIA

Apparently, the original meaning of "theoria," (*theôria*), which came to mean "contemplation," was the sending of state ambassadors (*theôroi*) to the oracles and games; *theôros*, in turn, has an uncertain derivation, but seems to be connected with *thea*, "seeing, looking at." A *theôros* would have been an official see-er, a looker-on at the games. *Thea*, for its part, has the same root as *theasthai* "gaze at, behold in awe or wonder," which in turn is to be related to *thauma* "wonder." "Theoria," with its cognate verb, *theôrein*, seems to have evolved in meaning from "sending an official see-er to the games," to "being a spectator at the games," to "being a spectator generally" (i.e., simply "seeing, viewing"), to "contemplating, contemplation."

In Book X of Aristotle's *Ethics* (the background of Plotinus' *Ennead* III, 8, 1–4: *vide supra* p. 127, n. 9) human beatitude is proved to consist in "theoria" or "theoretic activity" which is

. . . the best activity: for intellect (*nous*) is the best in us, and the best of knowables are those with which intellect is concerned. Again, it is the most continuous. For we are able to contemplate (*theôrein*) more continuously than to perform any practical activity whatsoever (*prattein hotioun*). And we think that pleasure is mingled with happiness; now, activity in accordance with wisdom is the most pleasant of the activities in accordance with virtues. For indeed the love of wisdom seems to have pleasures marvelous in purity and stability, but it is reasonable that those who know will pass their lives more pleasantly than those who seek.   (*Eth. Nic.* X, 8, 1177a19–27.)

Theoria is the activity of intellect, concerned with knowables; it is continuous and most pleasant. It is intellectual seeing, *knowing*, which is more pleasant than the search for knowing.

Similarly, for Aristotle in *Metaph.* Lambda, the life of a god, of an unmoved movent, is an act of knowing, a theoria, a contemplation (7, 1072b14–4). Therefore, when he says that a science "contemplates everything that is related to one physis," when he remarks that "grammar contemplates all articulate sounds," when he says that it is the province of one science "to contemplate opposites," when he says that it belongs to one science to "contemplate being *qua* being," etc., he is talking about knowing (*Metaph.* Gamma, 2, 1003b13–14; *ibid.* lines 19–21; *ibid.* 1003b34–1004a1). The English translations given for "theoria" in these and similar statements are misleading. Ross, for example, has "investigation" (1003b13–14), "investigates" (1003b19–21), "investigate" (1003b34–1004a1), "examine" (1005a2–3). Tredennick in these same places has "investigation," "studies," "study," "study." A science, an *epistême*, is for Aristotle not a consideration, but a knowing.[2]

If we call the "theoria" which Aristotle describes in all these passages "contemplation," we must use the word in a very exact sense. "Contemplation" can mean in English the act or state of considering, thinking over, mulling over—an act or state short of knowing. "Contemplation" of this sort is not Aristotle's "theoria."

In Plato also, "theoria" frequently appears to mean a permanent, stable knowing, an a-temporal "seeing" of an a-temporal object. (Cf. *Rep.* VI, 486 a; *ibid.* 517b–c)

NOTES

1. Cf. Joseph Owens, "Our Knowledge of Nature," in *Proceedings of the American Catholic Philosophical Association*, XXIX (1955), pp. 63–64; G.S. Kirk, *Heraclitus, the Cosmic Fragments* (Cambridge, England, 1954), p. 228.

2. Cf. Joseph Owens, *The Doctrine of Being in the Aristotelian Metaphysics* (Toronto, 1963), pp. 79–80.

INDEX OF PASSAGES CITED FROM THE ENNEADS